# YOU MAY FEEL A BIT OF PRESSURE

*observations from infertility's heart-wrenching ride*

Amy Gallo Ryan

*with a foreword by Lauren Smith Brody*

Attention schools and businesses: for discounted copies on large orders,
please contact the publisher directly.

For information contact:
Unsolicited Press
Portland, Oregon
www.unsolicitedpress.com
orders@unsolicitedpress.com
619–354–8005

Cover Design: Anne Pardes
Editor: Kristen Marckmann

ISBN: 978-1-963115-58-1

*For Tim*

"But in the end, stories are about one person saying to another: This is the way it feels to me. Can you understand what I'm saying? Does it also feel this way to you?"

*-Kazuo Ishiguro*

# Contents

# Praise for *You May Feel A Bit of Pressure*

"Amy Gallo Ryan's *You May Feel a Bit of Pressure* is a gift to women—those going through fertility struggles as well as anyone who wants to understand more of the roller coaster that is womanhood. At times heart-wrenching, Ryan's story is also reassuring, and her soothing voice offers a lovely dose of hope in a world where female viewpoints and experience do not often get their deserved air time. Honesty prevails—as do the nitty gritty details we all wonder about—in this heroic call to empathy."
— **Sarah Hoover, bestselling author of** *The Motherload*

"An unsparing, intimate and deeply honest account of infertility. For all the women out there who feel alone in their struggles—this book is your lifeline."
— **Jessica Zucker, PhD, author of** *Normalize It: Upending the Silence, Stigma, and Shame That Shape Women's Lives* **and** *I Had a Miscarriage: A Memoir, a Movement*

"This raw, honest, beautifully written memoir centers around Ryan's singular pursuit of giving birth to a child, and how infertility—and the loss of trust in her body—upends her very beliefs about herself. *You May Feel a Bit of Pressure* is as sharply observed as it is moving, buoyed by humor and grace. It will stay with me for a very long time."
— **Rae Meadows, author of** *Winterland*

"*You May Feel a Bit of Pressure* is a raw, rare window into the deep pain and endless hope of infertility, a brave and honest examination of the excruciating journey to motherhood and the love that endures it all."
— **Taylor Hahn, author of** *A Home for the Holidays*

introduce an audience to something otherwise completely foreign to them through the shared experience of vulnerability. Then you can zoom out, rally community, make sense of that hard time – and build support for progress – at scale.

With her own exquisitely sensitive telling of her story, Amy has – I just know it – written the book that will build community for anyone facing infertility and the people who love them and want to be on that island with them. Readers will find hope in these pages – but not just for the obvious thing you might imagine, a baby in arms by the end. It's something deeper: Hope that they will, one day, look in the mirror and see someone looking back at them who says: You are whole.

Lauren Smith Brody
Author and founder of *The Fifth Trimester*
Co-founder, Chamber of Mothers

# YOU MAY
# FEEL A BIT OF
# PRESSURE

## A note of clarification

Throughout this book I use the term IVF to refer to each of my attempts to get pregnant through in vitro fertilization, because that is the most accurate reflection of how it felt to me as a patient. Clinically, though, the procedures involving frozen embryos are called frozen embryo transfers, or FET.

# Anticipation

***

It could have been a cry that roused me, from asleep to awake in a single instant, the sort of soundless stirring only a mother can hear. It wasn't, though. Not yet. So I lay still as the Islamic call to prayer tremored, letting the words, the intonation, this unfamiliar lullaby return me to the world and the precise place I was in it. I wove my fingers together, palms kissing my belly, and closed my eyes, dreaming once again of the new life that would soon be twinkling on the other side of my skin.

When the call echoed in the daylight, lying on a dock in my sunny yellow bikini, I'd pause whenever the recording crackled, listen for a few moments, then return to my copy of *Gone Girl*. My husband, Tim, and I had been in Turkey for several days—first in Istanbul, now in Bodrum, the Turkish Riviera—but hearing the call broadcast every few hours still jolted me, reminding me that this seaside haven, arguably more beautiful than any other, held its own extra thrill of adventure for being nestled in a country that shared borders with Iraq, Iran, and Syria. Most of the time, it merely felt like paradise.

Just beyond our toes, the Aegean Sea shimmered, stunningly clear and quiet above its rock-studded floor. All around me were thick beds with plush cushions the color of oatmeal, arranged in groups along sun-bleached planks, each boasting a perfectly tanned, toned guest speaking French or Arabic, Turkish or Spanish, impossibly attractive humans who took turns executing cinematic half-moon dives into the sea, showcasing strong shoulders and impressive freestyle strokes before emerging to captivate Tim and me with a ritual they all practiced instinctively: The Suit Change. Each one exiting the water and tucking behind a curtained area to peel off soaking nylon and shimmy into dry swimwear, then laying the wet suit on the dock to bake in the sun before arranging themselves atop the day bed, saltwater droplets still glistening on skin. We exchanged an incredulous glance over the tops of our sunglasses: had we ever, in our standard summer getaways to the Jersey Shore, witnessed anything so chic? No, no we had not.

It was the sort of place where even the tiniest guests exuded sophistication: the beautiful, bobbling toddlers in various states of undress, the lanky grade school children huddled on their towels around a deck of cards. I splayed my book across my bare tummy and watched them, smiling; that was my future. Two months before boarding our flight to Turkey, where we'd traveled to celebrate our first wedding anniversary, I'd left my birth control to languish in the filled Rx bin at a CVS back in Manhattan. That makes it seem more offhanded than it was, as though my getting pregnant would be an unintended consequence of neglect, the contraceptive I couldn't be bothered to pick up. In fact, it was a choice. A thoughtful one. We had planned for this. We were ready. We were officially, excitedly trying for a baby. Which made this trip the most meaningful sort of occasion—a beginning and an ending all rolled into one.

Tim and I both knew that children would signal the end of our far-flung adventures. We loved traveling, and it had become our thing as a couple, together exploring the soaring granite of Yosemite, the richness of Spain, the submerged wonder surrounding Belize, the stirring soulfulness of the Serengeti. But babies were about to change all that. Of course they were, we understood how these things worked. There was an unconscious manual Tim and I shared, an internalized set of rules and dreams handed down to all of us kids raised in the comfort and security of

'80s suburbia. Go to college. Get a job. Fall in love. Start a family. Work hard, things work out. Truth was, we'd made it 31 years with little evidence suggesting otherwise. We'd attended college and met afterward as young graduates starting out in New York City. He'd since gotten a degree from Harvard Business School and was working his way up in the world of finance. I'd been an editor at Condé Nast, the most prestigious magazine company in the world, and was now working in digital media. Privilege does more than teach you that things work out; it often makes it so.

Now, we'd reached the next stage of programming, The Parenthood Years, which we'd watched so many friends and siblings embark on already. We'd observed, again and again, the messy wonder of creating a tiny nuclear family of one's own, growing surer at every turn that we wanted this for ourselves. To be upending our lives in the most permanent of ways was nerve-wracking and exhilarating. We couldn't wait.

There in Turkey, Tim's all-American charms seemed particularly poignant; flop of brown hair, compact build, a chest comprised of dueling plateaus in a shade of freckly pink that was as close to tan as he could get. His arms climaxed in a water balloon-sized bulge at the crook of each elbow; "You can't crush steel!" he liked to say back then, popping a fist brightly against a bicep, his green eyes reading almost amber with humor and sunlight. I rolled my eyes but laughed anyway. It was a dad joke in the making.

My body occupied nearly the same length of the chaise as Tim's, but often I'd sit up, cross-legged, shoulders hunched toward my book, fingers mindlessly searching through the underside of my top knot, feeling for my scalp. There was a linear quality to me, calves and forearms and neck, golden like a fig beneath the Turkish sun, all of it vertical except for the roundness around my bottom, which, in earnest, could only be described one way. I can't recall when I first heard of *childbearing hips*, whether it was an adult's misplaced remark about my teenage figure, or a descriptor I'd come across in a novel, tucking away the words that so clearly articulated the particular bowing of my body. Either way, that's what they were; wider than I'd like but built for something beautiful.

Reclining on the dock, lolling weightless in the sea, or perched at the bar, Tim and I talked as if we had just met, reminiscing about our wedding. "At this moment last year, we were…" I would say throughout the day, completing the sentence differently with each utterance, a private, nostalgia-themed Mad Lib.

We also imagined the future; nervous, giddy, disbelieving that we were on the brink of starting our family. Anticipating this new life in which we'd replace jet lag with the kind of exhaustion you can never quite sleep off. When would it happen, we wondered. How many kids would we have? (He made his case for three; I thought two or four). What would we name them? (Elijah for a boy, Tim suggested; I loved the simplicity of Sam). Would we raise them in New York City or move to the suburbs? Who would be the tougher parent? How would they change us? The answers beckoned, begging us to chase them down and solve the great mysteries of our lives.

Against the outrageous beauty of our current backdrop, these conversations felt more intimate than usual—our plans more tender. We were co-conspirators, imagining the less sexy family vacations of our future, far from the Aegean Sea. There was so much we wanted our kids to experience; ice cream bars from a boxy white truck that would melt faster than they could lick. The burn of saltwater shot up their little noses as a wave hurtled them toward shore. Falling asleep on a still summer night to the sound of crickets throbbing in unison. Standing around an open flame tending to marshmallows that wrinkled and shrank before collapsing between graham crackers. Hooded sweatshirts at sunset, damp, sandy suits worn all day long. A million tiny nothings that made up both of our ideas of childhood.

It was easy to dream of such things when our world seemed vast and vibrant, everything ahead of us. We were fortunate; tasting the exotic but choosing the ordinary. Which was just it; we still believed we got to choose the life, the future, the family we wanted.

The me I was back then, a young woman in a yellow bikini—relaxed, carefree, curious to discover the world—was still whole and filled with hope and optimism. She had it all figured out. That woman knew nothing of the me down the road, the jobless, baby-less me in stretched out yoga pants, who woke up most days with nowhere to go, her world shrunk to the four walls of an empty apartment where she sat hunched, laptop on thighs, Googling pregnancy symptoms for hours. *No implantation spotting, can I still be pregnant? Twinges in lower back 8 days post-ovulation mean anything? How early can you feel pregnancy symptoms? Slight cramping that goes away am I pregnant? Negative test 7 days post-transfer too early to tell?* That girl's eyes were hollow, scanning and searching until she was satisfied there was still a chance. Her nails were picked to nothing more than nubs, her arms track-marked like a junkie's from endless IVF blood draws.

Yellow Bikini Me was always up for an adventure.

She got one.

# *Optimism*

The bathroom of Cozy Riverside Cabin #5, tucked along Highway 89 in Livingston, Montana, was drab but clean, for the most part. The views from the adjacent bedroom, however, made this spot far superior to anywhere else I'd peed on a stick. The Absaroka Range stood silent and imposing all around us, and the Yellowstone River glittered down below.

Earlier in the trip, Tim and I had stopped for a drink at a cowboy bar that had been featured on the show *No Reservations*. Back when we'd taken in the scene from our couch, watching as Anthony Bourdain and the writer Jim Harrison sipped brown liquor there, the episode brought Montana to life for us; there were sweeping shots of spectacular ridges and verdant valleys, of horses clopping across rivers and gravelly, from-the-gut accounts of living life from locals who had undeniably done so. Still, all that cinematic glory did nothing to prepare me for how Montana actually felt, the wholeness of nature there, the astonishment of seeing it all exist so casually. Creamy lilac mountains taken in from the parking lot of the Missoula Safeway, simply a pleasant backdrop for buying milk.

There was a surreal sheen to everything in Montana. Nothing could quite be believed. And so it was, that in Montana, 50 miles from America's first national park, I got the one and only flashing positive ovulation test of my life. I held that plastic strip up high between my thighs until it was soaked through with urine, then rested it on the counter as usual. Only this time, when I went back to check, a convulsing smiley face had emerged, blinking up at me in crazed exultation. *Ho-ly shit.*

I'd been taking these tests for close to a year now, but virtually all I'd ever produced was a sad empty circle—not a smile, not even a face. A zero. And those zeroes were adding up. Ovulation tests are meant to be taken on consecutive days to identify a fertile window. For me, that meant virtually every morning, month after month, literally hundreds of days, I had kicked things off with a zero.

The only other smiley face I'd gotten was static instead of blinking, a glazed-over Stepford wife. But *this* smiley face, the *flashing* one, the one I'd only ever read about on the side of the box? She was here to tell me that my fertility was high (me! high fertility!) and better yet, that I had not yet peaked. With ovulation in sight but not imminent we had more days of trying, more opportunities for success, more favorable odds of getting pregnant. I never thought I'd see the day. But here we were, staying in a part of Montana called, of all things, Paradise Valley, and suddenly I had high fertility. It happened when we were actually, technically, in Paradise.

"Tim?" Excitement leaked from my voice as I emerged from the bathroom, holding up the stick like it was some sort of magic trick. "I can't believe it!"

"Yeah, baby!" Tim playfully swatted my butt. "Time to get down to business!"

We had just finished breakfast by the river and were back in our cabin packing and preparing to check out. Our plan had been to head to Bozeman, where we'd stroll around, then finish the drive to our last stop in Montana—a one-time cattle ranch turned lodge set amidst thousands of rugged acres. "I am seriously shocked," my brain was overloaded, each of my thoughts finding its way out of my mouth. "Do you think we should have sex right now? Or just wait? Maybe wait, I guess, the ranch looks amazing let's wait until we get there." As we giddily stuffed fleeces and hiking boots into our carry-ons, I checked the stick again and again to make sure I hadn't imagined it.

After all the months of zeroes, bringing the tests on this trip had, in itself, been a show of deluded optimism, but I had tucked them into my bag nonetheless, hauling them first to Santa Ynez, California, for my friend Kelly's wedding, then on to Montana. All for the virtually nonexistent chance that I would get to see that ecstatic cartoon grin. And, improbably enough, here she now was. As it turned out, my reproductive system was merely dormant, not dead. My body was quietly functional, more understated, less showy about releasing eggs, and you know what, I respected that. Perhaps Montana had resuscitated her with a few puffs of big sky air. Perhaps amidst the purity of grass and sky, mountains, prairies, and valleys, my anatomy had been compelled to perform its most fundamental functions, decided to answer its highest calling. I thought, and not for the first time on this trip, about my hair, a lightish brown with caramel streaks, which had looked its lifetime-best since we'd set foot out west. In air so clear and dry, my tight curls reflexively unclenched, settling into a more relaxed version of themselves. My ovaries, it seemed, were doing the same. *Montana*, I thought. *God bless you.*

We drove fast alongside the big rigs on the Interstate, singing along to country songs on the radio with our own impassioned renditions, a blur of green and brown and gold and blue out our windows. The final stretch was a long, lonely road, which led us to the ranch. In the hot stillness of a mid-September afternoon, we pulled up to a stunning beamed structure set amidst golden rolling hills and a sky that never stopped. Not a bad place to make a baby, I smiled to myself, grateful my body had gotten her shit together just in time. We would be the only guests on the entire property that first night, which the man at check-in let us know as he led us to our room, Tim and I exchanging a glance. We were officially all alone, in the middle of nowhere. The moment he left, Tim locked the door behind him, whipped the curtains across the wall of windows, and threw me atop the bed.

Afterward, I lay on the mussed sheets to give those wriggly sperm a chance to do their thing, unable to be anything but impossibly pleased with myself. Pleased and relieved; it was happening. I could exhale, be nowhere but here. When Tim sprang up, he headed to the closet, my guess was for a robe, though he found something else instead. "Pickles!" His term of endearment for me, though no part of my brain can recall its origin. "Hope you packed some heat, there's a gun safe in here!"

We dressed, pink-cheeked and ready to explore, and outside, as we strolled trails to nowhere, kicking up dust with our toes, I felt both small and enormously alive, my husband alongside me, each of us inside our own thoughts. The quiet was so quiet it echoed. Down a dirt path we found a pond, encircled by tall reeds that swayed in the breeze like a hula skirt. We inhaled the mountain air and sat in contented silence, trout plopping, my Montana hair dancing atop my shoulder blades in the sunlight.

Later that evening, a late summer storm rolled in, bringing swirling air, chunky rain, as Tim and I lingered over dinner. We watched for a while through the picture window before returning to our room to give it one more shot.

\*\*\*

Back in New York, I went into the long-awaited appointment to assess my fertility feeling almost sheepish, unsure if even being there was an overreaction: *So, yes, it's been a full year of trying, but as it turns out, my ovaries do work, they're just low-key about it, they have nothing to prove. But if you must know [looks down casually to inspect nails], I actually just ovulated on vacation. It's SO not a big deal. But I'm probably pregnant right now.* I stopped short of offering up the baby names already on a loop in my brain: Huck, in honor of the huckleberries that grew wild and plentiful out there, or Grey, borrowing from the name of that magical ranch in the middle of nowhere.

Except, by then, Montana's spell was broken.

The ultrasound technician let me know that I wasn't pregnant. The baby would be birthed only in my imagination. I left that day with a prescription in my pocket and a reality check.

Standing beneath some scaffolding outside, I called Tim to recap the results of the appointment. The good news, I offered, my voice breaking ever-so-slightly, was that I had a lot of eggs, constellations of them, clustered all over my ovaries. The bad news: I wasn't ovulating. The good-slash-bad news: Someone had finally acknowledged there was a problem.

In a way it was a relief to finally hear what I'd already known— that something was wrong. Despite the implication of all those zeroes I had been told to give it time—that since we were under the age of 35, we needed to have been trying to conceive for at least a year to meet the threshold of infertility, to even be *assessed*. These things can take a while, the doctors assured me. Try acupuncture. Be patient. Just relax. (Oh, so helpful—all of it). But now, finally, the burden of proof was off my shoulders. I could retire the cycle-charting workbook I'd been fruitlessly filling out for months, toss the remainder of the ovulation tests I'd been purchasing by the dozen. This new OB/GYN informed me that my ovaries were resisting ovulation. They weren't strong enough to produce a dominant follicle, and when they did, the egg that released wasn't of high enough quality to become a baby. But I could take a drug, Clomid, to stimulate ovulation and plump up one of my eggs so that one of Tim's sperm could zip its little way inside. It was hopeful news, in a sense: we would finally have a real chance.

I paused to let Tim, to let myself register the magnitude of the moment. We were closer to a baby than we had ever been. Yet in the span of that one appointment, we had gone from Normal

People Trying to Infertile Couple (though neither the doctor nor I had gone so far as to use that word). "This is a good thing," Tim insisted. "I know," I said, wiping away tears with the back of my hand, "it's just scary, you know? Once you acknowledge there's a problem you really have no clue how deep it goes."

That whole year of trying, Tim had been relentlessly pragmatic. He was a man who approached things mathematically, referencing the statistical chances of getting pregnant in any given month, reminding me that at some point the odds would be in our favor and it would happen. He used reason, urging me not to get ahead of myself with my concern and worry, not to indulge my worst fears about something really being wrong, his left brain hard at work trying to persuade my right brain, and all its creative machinations, to stop imagining dire outcomes. Tim was a solution-oriented person and this doctor's appointment satisfied his desire for a very rational next step. "It's going to be ok," he reassured me. "One hundred percent. It's going to happen."

For me, though, the long-held sense that we were biologically entitled to a baby was gone, and with it, the blind, naïve confidence that had allowed me to stride sure-footed through life. Once we moved into this shaky place, I began to absorb our newfound membership in a group for whom there are no guarantees. The question of having a baby had gone from when we would to how we would, with a terrifying word looming in the distance: *If* we would.

I can't recall if I was aware of it at the time, but the day back in Paradise Valley, when our luck seemed to have changed, happened to be Friday the 13th. That poetic moment, I didn't know at the time, would be our last go at a natural, unmedicated conception. Just a few days later, I began popping pills to help me ovulate and regulate my erratic cycles. If Montana was crisp mountain air sailing through my nostrils, these were straight-from-the-lab synthetics gulped down the throat.

But the truth was, Montana already felt like a dream. It's hard to hold on to the essence of something so pure in New York City, where there are conflicting, competing, chaotic demands for your attention at every turn. Aggressively honking yellow cabs. The stench of sidewalk trash. Bikers swiping you from every which way. Subway riders packed so densely you jerk this way and that, a single unit, as the train takes a curve, the flesh of strangers encroaching upon you from all sides. New York is a head-down kind of place; the sky exists, but you may only notice a slice of it between skyscrapers when a circling chopper commands that you look up.

So, I did what you do; I put my head down and got to it, popping my pills and focusing on work. I crammed into the F train each morning with my earphones in place to wall me off from the world, then joined my co-workers in our windowless strip of the office and, occasionally, in the (also windowless) conference room. It was urban life as usual, only now with fertility treatment as a footnote.

And so, life continued, as our old reality disappeared behind us and a new path unfurled. New Year's Eve. My second cycle on Clomid and the first-time I'd take a fertility shot of any kind. After an ultrasound the previous day, my OB/GYN had prescribed an injectable called Ovidrel to induce the release of my egg, thereby giving Tim and me a definitive 24-36-hour window to make a baby. We were intending to stay home that New Year's Eve anyway, but the Ovidrel injection gave us a purpose for being there. Suddenly a night-in felt like a plan, an event. I made Ina Garten's herbed pork tenderloin (fancy) and we drank champagne on the couch (extra fancy). As we toggled between countdown coverage, we decimated our joke of the night; "Different kind of shots this New Year's!" "Never thought this was the shot I'd be taking tonight!" (*Ba dum tss!*) There was levity and silliness and joy. We were happy to be home together, hopeful that this slight escalation in treatment, the act of penetrating my skin with a needle, would lead, finally, to the result we wanted. "It's kind of insane that they let people inject themselves with needles, don't you think," champagne fizzed in my brain as I lifted my shirt to expose the lower part of my belly. "I've got it," Tim's relentless confidence was powering us through. "Are you ready?" I grabbed a wad of flesh with two hands and steeled myself as he gave me a pre-injection three-count. "One…two…three."

***

It is only apparent to me in retrospect, but this was our personal point of no return. Up until then, events in my life could exist independently from the pursuit of pregnancy. Two months prior, my co-workers and I dressed as Kardashians for Halloween. Full stop. I don't know where I was in my cycle that day, or what appointment I may have been anticipating. But that night, on New Year's Eve, lines were crossed: the moment that separated one year from the next; the dermis protecting my blood and bones from a harsh world just beyond; the invisible boundary roping off fertility treatment from the rest of my life. In every instance, there was no going back.

In February, we spent a long weekend in Boston celebrating my college roommate's wedding, and though there were a million highlights—the wine-soaked rehearsal dinner, magical snowfall while getting ready with the bride, phenomenal after-party snacks—it is getting my period in the bathroom of Logan airport as we were set to depart, the thud of reality that our third round of Clomid had been unsuccessful, that colors my memory of the weekend.

Two months later, Tim and I invited our families for Easter: our first time hosting a holiday. I bought a cake plate and cloth napkins and tiny pastel egg candies that no one would eat but that looked pretty on the table. I soaked our wedding china in a sink full of soapy water so we could at long last peel off the price stickers. We brought all three sets of our parents together (no small feat), plus my sister and grandmother (*ten* people!), and we ate and drank and acted like grownups who lived in a real home equipped to entertain other grownups. But as soon as we had hugged and kissed goodbye, I succumbed to my urge to take a pregnancy test. The agony of not being pregnant is what I remember most about that day.

For me, real life had become intertwined with fertility life, the footnote becoming the headline. I didn't know it then, but I was speeding toward a moment when real life would be overtaken entirely; when treatment would be all that remained.

***

Before long we had graduated to the next level of intervention, Intrauterine Insemination (IUI), in which my follicles were stimulated with Clomid and Tim's sperm injected with the proverbial turkey baster to increase the odds for fertilization. When that didn't work, the OB/GYN let me know it was about time we make our way to a fertility specialist. It was under his care that we tried a couple more cycles of IUI, and eventually graduated to in vitro fertilization (IVF).

The whole way through, I mourned the loss of a simple thread of optimism I had taken for granted: that I would get pregnant naturally. Doing it any other way felt directly in opposition to the kind of mother I hoped to be. I had always imagined that some greater power—fate, God, the universe—would determine which of Tim's millions of sperm cells would find its way inside one of my eggs and decide the folds of our child's ear lobes, the curve of her smile, the exact arc of his tiny toes. I wanted to push out our baby and I wanted to do it naturally, meaning drug-free, squeezing shut my eyes and bearing down during the excruciating ascent of each contraction. I wanted to breastfeed, bonding with and nourishing our baby as mothers have done as long as human beings have walked this earth. As someone who finds comfort in the idea that things naturally play out as they're meant to, who had been raised to cultivate physical and mental toughness, refusing to pop so much as a Tylenol for the artificiality it would introduce into my bloodstream, my stripped-down vision of pregnancy and motherhood made sense. But I also wanted to go natural because I wanted to be *a* natural.

Easy, patient, gentle, loving, I aimed to embody the ideal, impossible version of a mother—one with a baby strapped to her chest, effortlessly in tune with my infant's every tiny whimper and cry, my soothing jiggle or caress in response intuitive, knowing, warm. Yet there I was, incapable of taking the very first step.

It was a meaningful loss, that I wasn't some earth mother able to effortlessly conceive a baby. And yet when the moment for IVF neared, in a perverse way, I couldn't wait. One of my most deeply-held delusions, my most dangerous dances with optimism, was that IVF was an ace in the hole.

Think about it—we would be stimulating my ovaries with a strict protocol of daily shots, goading them into producing as many large follicles as possible. After about two weeks, once those eggs grew to a precise and ideal size, they would be suctioned out of my body so that a doctor could attempt to fertilize each individually with a solitary sperm, a process known as Intracytoplasmic Sperm Injection (ICSI). The ones that fertilized would then be monitored, and the resulting embryos that continued to grow would either be transferred back into my uterus or frozen to use later.

When the packages of syringes and alcohol swabs, an injectable pen, bandages, medication vials, along with one of those red biohazard boxes you see at the doctor's office arrived, commandeering our kitchen counter where Ina's glorious pork tenderloin had so recently rested, I was strangely exhilarated. *This is serious*, the drugs seemed to say. This was specialty pharmacy shit; complex layers of follicle-stimulating and egg-releasing and hormone-regulating drugs designed to be injected through specific body parts—this one through the fat below my belly button, that one into the top corner of my butt cheek—at specific times of day. This was no summer storm on a ranch in Montana—nothing wistful or romantic or natural or poetic. This was a serious treatment plan and this, I was sure, would work.

That was the thrilling part: my certainty. Maybe I was naïve, or ignorant, or caught up in the relentlessly positive prognosis I consistently heard from my doctors, or maybe most uninitiated couples believe what I did: that IVF works.

Fueled by that certainty, I threw myself into the rigors of the cycle, allowing treatment to bleed even deeper into the main frame of my life. No, I can't get after-work drinks tonight, or the night after, or the one after that; I have to go home for my shots. At work, a video shoot outside the city was scheduled toward the end of my cycle. No, I can't travel there a day early; instead, I stayed, beholden to morning monitoring, then commuted two-and-a-half hours out the day of the shoot, and two-and-a-half hours back that evening so Tim could shoot me up with meds.

The day of the embryo transfer, Tim and I sat in the transitional space that comes after the waiting room but before the procedure location, as he stretched his arm out in front of us to snap a selfie. In my starchy hospital gown, my hair looped beneath the synthetic fibers of a blue net, I gamely smiled into his phone. We already knew that the cycle had been, by all accounts, extremely successful, my body responding beautifully at every turn. That first stimulation yielded 19 mature eggs, 12 of which fertilized and seven of which grew to the blastocyst stage; all robust, viable, exquisite clusters of cells. Embryos; microscopic babies-to-be. And today, we would transfer the most promising one back into my uterus.

In the picture, Tim looks youthful, excited; I look a little weary, maybe, but full of hope. The mere fact of the picture's existence reveals our frame of mind: This was it. The day I got pregnant.

After the transfer I was wheeled to the recovery area and left to lay flat for 30 minutes. When it was time to dress and leave, I walked slowly, gingerly, as pregnant women do. Out front, Tim hailed a cab while I clutched a plastic card; it showed an orb containing many smaller orbs inside. The first image of our baby.

We got our results nine days later, the morning after Father's Day. No selfies were taken.

*** 

To have rational, reasonable thoughts, you must exist in the real world. I did not. Fertility had, by now, wholly subsumed my life. I was also in a state of shock: IVF not working had been unthinkable. And so it was in this headspace that I decided to quit my job. That was just for starters. After that, I decided that we would purchase and renovate an 11-bedroom, in-need-of-love lodge on a tiny island in Seeley Lake, Montana, move there, and run it ourselves.

Let me explain.

Within days of that first IVF, we had decided to take the summer off from treatment. It was mid-June, and instead of relief, there was suddenly a vacuum in my racing, anxious mind. Until now there had always been a next step to research, to prepare for: I'll take my temperature and chart my cycles. After that I'll try acupuncture. Then we'll move on to medication. After a month of Clomid we'll do another round and another and another. Next, we'll try IUI. After that we'll switch to a fertility specialist. Next, we'll do IVF. And then I'll be pregnant. Only I wasn't. What now?

It came to me on a blistering, sunny day over July 4th weekend, on the beach in Charlestown, Rhode Island, visiting Tim's family. Plopped in my beach chair, legs splayed in front of me, I picked up my phone to find a text from Desi, one of my closest friends and the person responsible for igniting my interest in Montana. He had been born and raised in Missoula, and from the time we met in New York City the summer after we graduated college, all I had ever heard from him was how much he couldn't wait to move back. When Tim and I planned our visit out west, Desi made a special trip home to show us around.

The text from Desi that day went something like this: *Holy shit, look what's for sale!!!!!!!!* And included a link to an article about how the University of Montana was selling off a very unique property called Montana Island Lodge. Before I'd even clicked through, I was aware that suddenly the whole world felt different, more like someplace I wanted to be.

When we'd touched down in Missoula the previous summer, Desi had picked us up at the airport so we could drive directly to his family's cabin near Seeley Lake, and on the way, he had something to show us. "You have to see this place, it's insane," Desi began, as we curved around glorious Salmon Lake and a sprawling, rustic structure on a tiny island came into view. I'd never seen anything like it, save for possibly in a movie, and this house, Montana Island Lodge, had plot twists to spare. Desi went on to regale us with the shockingly grim history of the place: the millionaire inventor who financed it with a fortune built from, of all impossibly ironic things, the contraceptive sponge, followed by a tragic accident, a yacht set on fire, and a death by suicide. Wide-eyed, Tim and I hung on every word as we gazed at the peaceful view. I turned my head as we passed to watch it all vanish behind us, then never thought of it again.

Now all these months later, on the sand in Rhode Island, I was reading how the University of Montana was putting the lodge up for sale. I swiped furiously through the slideshow, taking in the natural glory of the outside—the sweeping porches, the lakefront dock, the towering pines—along with the cavernous, beamed ceilings and '80s décor that defined the interior. It was massive but cozy. Grand yet simple. Picturesque, secluded, hugged by tall trees and clear, cold lake in all directions. It was unfiltered Montana magic. The article noted that the University had used it for retreats and run it as a lodge, pointing out that such a specific type of property would require a specific type of buyer. *Us!* I was rocketed out of my IVF fog. *We were the buyer!*

My thoughts unspooled rapidly. Never mind that our trip 10 months prior was the first and only time Tim and I had set foot in Montana. Or that we had no family or friends in-state save Desi's parents. This was a once-in-a-lifetime opportunity to do something incredible. To have a real adventure. To live the plot of a Hallmark Christmas movie! Tim was a business guy, he would figure out how to make the lodge profitable. I was creative and visual and could oversee the renovations and décor updates, then get us press through my magazine contacts in New York. We'd wear plaid and build fires and turn the place around, welcome guests, infuse warmth, create life. And then we'd *actually* create life; we'd have a baby, a Montana baby, and she'd grow up barefoot in the cool shade beneath the pines in summer, bundled in down in winter as I pulled her on a sled over the frozen lake. We'd need to talk the university down on price, of course, but they were motivated to sell, and it was such an unusual place, I doubted they were getting lots of bites.

I handed over my phone to Tim so he could read the article. "Remember? That crazy house on the lake?" I prompted.

"I guess so," my phone was already being returned.

"I think we should buy it." Tim's face broke into a bemused smile. "I'm completely serious," I said, and started to outline all my points. "I have zero doubt that we could make that place a really cool travel destination, and I honestly think as a business it would be successful. Who wouldn't want to stay there?" Tim listened to my oration there on the beach, but it wasn't until we were in the car driving back to New York that I really got going, borrowing from any number of city-folk-choose-happiness-and-become-innkeepers scripts. Sandy toes propped on the dash I rattled off all my thoughts, about how happy we'd been in Montana, how that slower, simpler life would really suit us. Sure, it was absurd, I acknowledged, but why couldn't we make it real? We needed to *do something*. We needed change. We needed to move forward, to take control, to alter the coordinates of our life in some way. We had thought a baby would be the thing to do it, but maybe we needed to make other decisions, focus our attention elsewhere, and then the baby would come, too. Perhaps, it occurred to me, Tim had never seen a Hallmark Christmas movie. Perhaps he didn't realize that organizing your life into the approximation of a snow globe is how one is guaranteed to live happily ever after.

I interpreted Tim's listening, his patience in hearing me out, as interest, and I felt elated and further emboldened by the fact that my arguments seemed to be swaying him. Looking back, his silence, surely, was an expression of relief. This particular delusion had breathed life back into me. I felt passion, saw promise, was capable of caring about something other than trying to get pregnant (though, of course, that was part of the fantasy too). Whatever it was that inspired it, Tim not only didn't shut me down, he encouraged me to take it a step further. "If you're so interested, why don't you email the listing agent?"

That was all I needed to hear.

*** 

My line of thinking may have been delusional, but my thoughts were sharp and in focus. It was as if a million fantasies I'd harbored over the course of my life converged, causing a powerful chemical reaction that crystallized their celestial ether into a different substance entirely. My living-in-the-woods fantasies, born from my childhood days picking blueberries and sleeping in a cabin at summer camp; daydreams of nature in its purest iteration, which I applied as homeopathic balm for the chronic affliction that is New York City; the temptation of escape taken to the extreme—I was already isolated because of infertility, now I could disappear to an actual, literal island. All of it suddenly seemed possible.

The next day I sent a message to express our interest in Montana Island Lodge, request some tax and financial information, and ask a few nuts-and-bolts questions. When Kevin (but, let's be real, possibly Santa Claus in disguise?), wrote back, I was ecstatic. Kevin was taking me seriously, treating me as an actual, potential buyer. We went back and forth, Tim chiming in to ask specific questions about profitability, occupancy, the logistical implications of the lake freezing over in winter. Kevin sent us tax data and spreadsheets detailing the revenue analysis and business patterns. It all felt so real. And why couldn't it be? People did these things. They took risks, they pushed themselves past the boundaries of logic. Could we talk them (way) down on price? Could we get a loan, borrow money from our parents? Could we make this work?

For weeks I went on like this, whipping around within a funnel cloud of deluded optimism, a Montana summer storm of my own making. At night, after work, I wanted to talk about the lodge. I proposed flying to Missoula so we could visit the property, fall in love with it in autumn. Get a sense of how it felt to sit on the porch with a cup of coffee, how the air smelled first thing in the morning, what the lapping lake sounded like as we were drifting off to sleep.

The end came softly—nothing like the harsh and final rush of blood in your underpants. The lodge cost millions of dollars and we didn't have millions of dollars. Tim, with gentleness and grace, pulled me back to earth. It wasn't going to happen. It didn't make sense. We couldn't afford it. Not even close. But—maybe it wouldn't sell, and they'd reduce the ask significantly. Tim emailed Kevin to put an end to our inquiry, stating that if the sellers moved on price to let us know. His willingness to join me in my madness, then leave the door open that tiny sliver, felt like deep, real love.

We had gotten our hopes up so many times over the past few years, I'd become well-practiced at letting things go. The property would not be the thing to save us, but enough days had passed, I had survived on the notion of Montana Island Lodge for the better part of a month, and we were now far enough into the future so that I could see IVF on the horizon again. It was August: we'd be starting back up in just a few weeks.

In the years since, I've only recently returned to Montana. The place we almost made our baby, the place we almost remade our lives. I don't know if I ever did ovulate there, if that test result was real, or whether Montana was, in fact, the reason for it. Those may very well have been gateway delusions, clearing the path for the one about how we'd buy the multimillion-dollar lodge and start a new life. I guess beneath that sky, so clear, so limitless, you can't help but dream big enough to fill it.

# Betrayal

***

*"I don't want the fucking orange juice."*

It was the middle of the night, but my dad's voice—its untamed vitriol, the distinct veil of otherness—awakened all of my senses immediately. I knew in an instant what kind of scene we were living.

When you are a kid with a type 1 diabetic parent, a fear of the unseen, of unpredictable, imperceptible shifts within the body, is always there. Whenever my dad's blood sugar would bottom out, whenever he would "get low," there was almost never a warning. One moment he was his formidable, stoic self, the next he had the cognition of a child, speaking nonsensically, behaving erratically, storming through the house with a terrifying purposelessness as my mother chased him around with a glass of OJ, pulpy liquid sloshing over the sides.

My father himself could surely feel a diabetic shock approaching, he had spent decades finely attuning his senses to what a dip in insulin felt like. It was a private superpower he possessed, one the world would never appreciate. He spent probably 362 days a year administering a command over his body, recalibrating his blood sugar with precision, pricking his finger before every glass of wine and after every round of golf, keeping a log, in his clipped shorthand, of every meal, every bologna sandwich and bowl of minestrone, along with its resultant blood sugar reading. He was vigilant—hyper-controlling—about threading the needle, and he was almost always successful at regulating his system before the shock claimed his senses. But when his body got away from him, when he didn't catch it in time, our entire family lapsed into chaos.

On this particular night, the scene unfolded long after we had all gone to bed, light switches being flicked hurriedly, the tail of a comet shooting across our dark house. Beneath my dad's gruff, barking profanity there was a cloudiness that was unmistakable. I crept out my door and met my sister in silence at the top of the stairs. He was refusing the sugar, as he sometimes did, because he was too deep inside the shock to understand that he needed it. In these cases, my mom would have offered something else—a coke, a hard candy—trying and trying until he would accept some form of the sweetness that would bring him back. This night it took awhile, long enough that my mother called the police. That was unusual, even unprecedented. An episode could usually be resolved quickly; it was rare for him to resist this way. But on this night, as the yelling continued and the minutes ticked by, she must have felt she needed reinforcements.

I cannot recall whether my dad finally relented before or after the officer arrived, his unintelligible fury finally subdued by a warm rush of sugar. What I do remember is sitting on the steps so that my body remained in the shadows but my eyes, peering through the slats of the banister, could take in the view of a policeman in our living room, urging my dad to calm down. The broad shoulders, the navy uniform, the image of authority greater than my father's, set against the backdrop of our faded loveseat and antique piano, seared itself into my memory on sight.

When it was all over and the invisible beast within my dad had been tamed, I followed my sister into her room so I could spend the rest of the night snuggled beside her. But first I hovered at her window, peeking out from the side of the shade to watch the patrol car pull out of our driveway and into the stillness of our cul-de-sac, to be erased by the dark night.

42

Which is to say I've known almost my whole life that the body has whims of its own. This has always frightened me. A staid suburban home thrust into upheaval without warning. Police lights flashing in the driveway when you didn't know to expect them.

*** 

Most afternoons, certainly by 5 p.m., the worn wooden floor of my office began to vibrate. The wellness website where I worked was part of a luxury health and fitness club, and my desk was located above one of the company's workout spaces in Manhattan where the sheer number of sneakered feet pounding on treadmills—bodies hurtling through space—actually shook the building.

Bodies were our business at this company; crafting them, nourishing them, celebrating them. After spending nearly six years as an editor at a magazine focused on women's health and fitness, it was familiar terrain. I was neither an exercise-junkie nor a health-nut, yet somehow I had carved out a career sharing truths about muscle fibers and nutrient absorption, the secret to clear skin and how to tame hormones gone haywire, all the inner workings and outer adornment of the human body. I liked to think I knew my stuff.

So when Liz, a friend from my old magazine days who was now running the website managed to stump me with a question about my own body, I was caught off guard. "Do you know when you're ovulating?" she had asked, our chairs swiveled to face each other in the open-concept workspace. "Like, can you feel it?" She was asking because she knew Tim and I had been trying to get pregnant for a few months now, and she was also aware that nothing had happened yet. I had shared our baby-making plans with her—with lots of friends—openly, excitedly, unthinkingly, because I was confident that it would happen for us eventually, and it all seemed so matter-of-fact. My answer? "Oh, I absolutely cannot feel it," said with a jokey lightheartedness that in no way reflected how I really felt. Liz didn't seem surprised, necessarily, but she told me she could feel it. Unequivocally. Our friend Vickie walked by and joined the conversation; she could feel it too. *What was anyone even talking about?* The notion of *feeling* ovulation had never so much as occurred to me. I couldn't imagine the sensation of an egg releasing: Was it like a snowflake gliding? A pinball rolling? An innocuous ache? The teensiest twitch? "I have no idea when I'm ovulating," I admitted, the ground trembling beneath my feet. Apparently, unbeknownst to me, knowing when one was ovulating was the most obvious thing in the world. I decided it was time to pay attention.

I had always felt connected to my body—or, rather, very much inside of it. There was nothing to connect to exactly because I was my body and my body was me. Growing up, I watched as it performed so many casual miracles; skinned knees that gushed red then fused neatly back together; stringy arms somehow strong enough to hoist me up the ropes in gym class; the achy, angst-y first period that showed up on cue amidst the agony of middle school. In my late 20s, I completed my first New York City Marathon, which introduced me to the outer limits of my body's capabilities. I'd learned from experience that in a matter of months, I could coax my body, train it, push it from a start/stop three-mile jog to an exhilarating 26.2. How extraordinary.

So when it came to having a baby, I took for granted that my body would show up for me as it always had, an assumption supported by three-decades of experience. The same month I stopped taking birth control I bought my first jar of prenatal vitamins. *And away we go!*

***

The night Hurricane Sandy made landfall on the east coast, Tim and I were holed up in our apartment, eating spaghetti and drinking red wine. The subways had closed at 5 p.m. the previous evening, and with our offices inaccessible and New York City all but shut down, we'd spent the day close to our downtown Manhattan apartment, stocking up on energy bars and tracking the storm on CNN. When the lights cut out around 9 p.m., water pelting our windows, we cracked another bottle of wine and settled in on the floor. Candles lit, fluffy, leopard-print throw spread out on the parquet, we sat around my fully charged laptop and sang, then danced our way through my iTunes library. Arcade Fire, Ben Harper, Bruce Springsteen. *Hey, little girl, is your daddy home? Did he go and leave you all alone? I got a bad desire. Oh, oh, oh, I'm on fire.* One by one our devices succumbed to exhaustion—two phones, a computer—and all sound, all connection, was swallowed by darkness. Lips stained, we finished our wine and took in the scene out our picture window; a lower Manhattan without a single twinkling tower, blank traffic lights whipping around, dangling over shadowy, flooded streets.

Riding out that historic hurricane together, feeling apprehensive on the 10th floor of a city so unusually dark and still, imagining our windows shattering from high winds or flying debris felt sexy and scary, our senses heightened by the ferocity of the storm, then relaxed by alcohol; our bodies close together in the dark. When we finally fumbled into the bedroom, giggling, drunk and a bit disoriented, it felt easy to begin kissing, rolling, groping as the rain clattered on. If I was ovulating at the time, I didn't know about it. This was nearly a year before Montana, back when I couldn't be bothered to track my cycle. I still believed that spontaneous, random sex could result in a baby. Perhaps, I imagined, still prey to romantic thoughts about how this all would go, we'd even have a hurricane baby.

As it turned out, that night yielded tremendous destruction along the east coast, including the worst flooding New York City had seen in hundreds of years. It also led to an inundation of babies born nine months later, as I read in the *New York Times* the following summer. Ours, however, was not one of them, and long after the lights came back on, I was still very much in the dark about why I wasn't getting pregnant. I still could neither feel nor detect ovulation, and my once-predictable periods had become reliably irregular, vacillating between 32 and 56 days in any given cycle. I read a book that advised me to monitor my morning temperature; in tracking its dips and peaks I'd be able to discern when an egg had just been released. Each day the thermometer was nestled beneath my tongue before my feet even touched the floor.

But my temperature patterns were irregular, too. Which was confounding. I was aware that many women faced challenges conceiving, of course, but my body had never given me reason to consider that I would be among them, especially since fertility-wise, I was on the right side of 35. But there were too many inconsistencies to ignore, and nine months off birth control seemed like a reasonable enough stretch to see an OB/GYN without it being an overreaction. Which it wasn't, I reminded myself. This was merely due diligence.

"I don't think you have anything to worry about," shrugged the doctor after hearing my concerns and completing a brief examination. "Women expect it to happen right away, but just give it time. You're only 31, it's only been a few months, and you really have plenty of time." It was a vaguely medical translation of *be patient, sweetie*; she may as well have yawned. "If nothing happens after a full year then come back and we can take a closer look. In the meantime, you can always try acupuncture, anecdotally that can sometimes help get things going." "Oh, really?" I replied with nonchalance in the exam room, as though I was as bored by this conversation as she was. Back at my desk I immediately shared what I'd learned with Liz, who knew of someone in the office with a great acupuncturist. I got the recommendation and scheduled my first session. *Bada bing!* I applauded my take-charge attitude. *Making shit happen.*

A few days later, dozens of acupuncture needles were pierced through the skin of my belly, each silver spear its own question—

*hello? anyone there?*—to which my inner matter responded with a microscopic spasm, again and again, like the sensation of fingers snapping drilled down to the head of a pin. *Yes, here!* Once the insertion was complete and needles dotted my stomach, the acupuncturist placed a heat lamp over me and left the room. I felt more in control of my body than I had in months. I was enlivened, finally able to *do something*, and I took pleasure in envisioning what was happening inside; blockages dislodging and blood rushing, cells plumping up like tiny balloons, ovaries pulsing to life. I imagined swirls of red as my inner wasteland transformed into a rich and fertile home where our baby could grow.

My body and I had entered a new era of our relationship, defined, paradoxically, by awareness and discord, my attention hyper-focused on daily temperature readings and ovulation tests telling me when I *should* have sex, rather than tuning into the more intimate signals my body used to send when I craved it. "Tonight, we will be having sex! (And probably tomorrow too,)" I wrote to Tim over email during the workday, not bothering to make the invitation more titillating beyond the exclamation point to convince him it would be fun (!!!). "Can't wait!" he would reply, both of us choosing to ignore the obvious sub-optimal realities of planned sex. It was a new era for us, one where the ambiguities of desire, where mundane moments seemed to flow organically and surprisingly into passionate ones, had become irrelevant. It didn't matter when we were moved to approach each other's bodies. We now showed up for predetermined appointments. (Yay!)

As our sex lost its spontaneity, it became bloated with significance. Every encounter had the potential to be *the* time, an awareness I found impossible to set aside. Whatever part of the brain processes primal pleasure now faced competition from the part that was determined to have the kind of otherworldly sex worthy of producing our first-born child. It was an impossible paradigm: scheduled sex that, somehow, must also be extraordinary.

Month after month we engaged in this ritual; weeks of temperature-readings, cycle-charting, ovulation test-taking, and acupuncture-poking, all of which built up to the climax—a few nights of strategically-scheduled sex—which Tim began unceremoniously referring to as 'Business Time.' If that sounds depressingly dispassionate, reeking of work and obligation, calling to mind sad skirt suits and office supplies, I swear it felt affectionate. As in, "You ready to get down to business?" asked with a wide grin and a double-handed grab of my butt. Or, "I'm about to give you the business," whispered in my ear as we started kissing. "Business time tonight?" was a frequent text exchanged as the term became part of our private shorthand—an intimate, jokey, non-sexual way to talk about our sex life. We had never had a need for such language before because we never talked much about sex—we just did it. Now, a year and a half into our married life, that had changed. Business, oddly enough, was an appropriate term for what was happening. We had become partners in our own little start-up; an aspiring mom-and-pop shop, so to speak.

In the course of all this fruitless trying—the business of attempting and failing to get pregnant—I began to feel my body slip away from me. I pictured my active external self, rosy-cheeked and bright-eyed after a run as fraudulent, housing a lifeless reproductive system within, a bunch of defunct organs clustered in the shadows, collecting cobwebs. That trust between my body and me, so implicit I'd never noticed it, eroded at the precise moment I became aware of its existence. I had come to think of my body as an objective entity to be tested and treated and managed and dealt with. My body was no longer *me*.

Throughout each stage of medical intervention, as things seemed so promising month after month, the mystery of it all burned me up. My rational brain was desperate for answers, but a diagnosis continued to elude us. There was no *here's the problem and here's how we're going to fix it*. My infertility was unexplained. My ovaries and uterus *should* have been working—they just weren't. Which, to me, implied that my body was choosing this. It was letting me down. Making me suffer.

Undeterred, I continued my efforts to persuade it. During my first round of IVF, I gave up coffee and alcohol in hopes of producing the strongest embryos and healthiest pregnancy possible. I felt clean and virtuous—was I starting to resemble an enlightened yogi? Or possibly even Gwyneth Paltrow?— sipping lemon water and hot herbal tea, mentally clear and physically buoyant despite the 19 rapidly growing eggs jostling for space among my reproductive organs.

The purging, however, was not enough; it was on a Monday morning in mid-June, while at work, when I got the call. I ducked out to speak to the nurse, then returned an hour later, blotches of red mapped across my face. My colleague, Ashley, watched me as I walked in and avoided her gaze. "Do you want wine?" she offered. "Let's go drink wine." Her invitation hung in the air for a moment. "Maybe," I said. "I don't know." I collapsed into my chair where I remained for a few minutes, barely capable of logging into my computer, unable to remember the stories I was supposed to edit that day. "Yes," I said finally. "I want wine." And so my friends put their work aside, gathered me up, and walked me to the elevator where I angled myself toward a corner, hoping no one would notice us. "Can I give you a hug?" Sheila asked as we waited in silence. I opened my arms to her, and she held me tight.

Four of us strolled down Broadway, nudging through the lunchtime throng into an open-air bistro in the middle of Union Square where we were greeted by ceiling fans and leafy plants and, most importantly, rosé. We sipped tentatively at first, ladies whose lunches typically entailed a workout and a bowl of lettuce next to our keyboards. But then we found our groove. A while later, check paid but not yet ready to leave, we emerged into the sizzling city afternoon and slid into the sidewalk seating out front where we asked for another bottle.

It had been a month since I'd had a sip of alcohol and I wanted it to feel—momentous? Cathartic? Something. Isn't that what people did, when something excruciating happened—drink to blunt their feelings, or to underscore them, or to honor the heartbreak through some grandiose moment of drunkenness? It didn't feel grand, though. It felt so terribly sad.

At least the rosé succeeded in keeping me in one place, anchored by the company of friends so that I wouldn't have to be adrift at my desk pretending to work or alone in my apartment. Our team operated autonomously, there was no one looking for us, so in the glare of that Monday afternoon, I drank and drank, discussing Ashley's upcoming wedding, the Real Housewives of whatever city, all the things pissing us off at work. My friends distracted me until I was joylessly drunk and the afternoon had passed. It was finally time to go home and meet Tim at our apartment.

Three days later, Tim and I took the 45-minute flight to Martha's Vineyard for an unintentionally well-timed long weekend away. We stayed in a pink gingerbread inn with a wraparound porch, not far from the downtown of Oak Bluffs. When we strolled out in search of coffee and breakfast that first morning, I found unexpected healing in the form of an iced coffee with almond milk from a charming local shop called Beetlebung. I had missed my morning coffee throughout the cycle—the taste, the ritual, the way it tugged on the corners of my mind until the slackness of sleep was pulled taut and the day calibrated and settled into place. Something about this particular cold, milky, caffeinated beverage sliding over and around the ice packed inside the plastic cup, sipped in the morning shade on this quiet, sunshine-y island brought me peace. It brought my world into focus. Whether it was the drink, the place, or the time that had passed, I felt that everything was going to be all right.

We began each of our lazy days on Martha's Vineyard at Beetlebung, sublime iced coffees reminding me of myself, then made our way around the island—to an empty stretch of sand in Oak Bluffs, a guts-stained dock in the fishing village of Menemsha, a harborside bar overlooking bobbing boats and the island of Chappaquiddick. In moments of stillness, Tim and I staring out at the ocean, one of us would ask, "What are we going to do?" unsure how to start this conversation we'd never imagined having. "Your body needs a break," Tim said. "I think we should take a break and come back to it fresh in a couple of months." Between Clomid, IUIs, and IVF we had done seven consecutive medicated cycles—it had been a lot. "I agree," I said softly. "Let's take a break for the summer."

Which, it should be said, was my intention. It really was. I just didn't know how. I was gripped by infertility—the infuriating, soul-crushing, diabolical mystery of it all—and I was convinced that if I only tried things just a little bit differently, I could get it all under control. Despite what we'd agreed, I did the opposite of taking a break: I tried harder. I had always believed that whatever it was I was after—the A on an exam, a faster mile—that hard work could get me there. Head-down determination was reliable in a way that my body, seemingly, was not. So if my body didn't want to do its job, then I would push (read: force) it along. Give it no other choice. Within weeks of that first failed IVF cycle, I'd quit my job to reduce stress and focus on the process. I would no longer produce stories about the human body in general; I was dedicating myself to the well-being of only one.

I'd brought up leaving my job before, frustrated that my background in lifestyle writing made me feel useless and unseen at a place so obsessed with fitness. Everything I did there felt imbued with failure and, when taken alongside my ongoing failure to get pregnant, it all began to take its toll. The painful irony of being hyper-focused on bodies for a living, as I happened to be losing faith in my own—that didn't help either. Whenever I voiced my thoughts about leaving, though, Tim was quick to talk some sense into me. "What would you do instead?" he'd ask. "You can't leave without having something else lined up, you'd be miserable not working." But after IVF, as we began to appreciate our infertility as more complex than we had previously understood, I blamed the stress and unhappiness of my job for all of it. "If this job is responsible in any way for what is happening inside my body, then I owe it to myself to walk away." Tim listened, and this time, he replied differently. "If you want to quit then I think you should do it," he said simply. Suddenly, it was real.

I gave my notice to Liz, but avoided telling most people I was leaving, letting them learn the news when I sent my goodbye email as one foot was already out the door. I wanted to be invisible, sneaking out unnoticed just as I had the day we drowned ourselves in rosé. *Please don't look at me*, I willed silently. *Please don't ask questions.*

When we resumed treatment, giving up booze and caffeine would be the least of my efforts, I vowed. This time, to wrest total control over my body, I would go full Gwyneth; I would give up sugar and soy and dairy and non-whole grains. I switched to natural beauty products. I purged our apartment of harsh cleaning agents that might be interfering with my endocrine system and messing with my hormones. I continued to go to acupuncture. I drank teas to support fertility and ate bee pollen to fortify my reproductive organs. I exercised, but gently, resting in between. I did yoga, channeling intention and positive energy into my fertility. I tried Reiki, a form of energy healing, and Gua Sha, where skin is scraped with a special tool to improve circulation (like I said: *full motherfucking Gwyneth*). On one occasion my acupuncturist inserted needles with miniature herb bundles at the top, later lighting those on fire in an ancient form of heat therapy called moxibustion. I rode the subway home smelling like I'd just gotten stoned, but I didn't care. I'd do, try, sacrifice anything.

Depriving myself of the simple pleasures I had always enjoyed and the career I had busted my ass to build may not have been fun, but it was surprisingly easy. I almost relished it. As I saw it, this was my first test of maternal sacrifice. I was doting on my body, giving up everything in its name, which proved I could give up whatever was necessary for the well-being of my child. I felt sure this inner cleansing would be the thing to make the difference, and I felt righteous to be proving myself worthy of motherhood. I was *earning* my pregnancy.

I'd always been focused, determined, but the single-mindedness with which I pursued my goal was beyond anything I could have imagined. A realization, gestating for some time now so to speak, had finally crystallized within me: There was nothing I wanted more than I wanted to be a mother. Having children had always seemed like an implied part of my future, something I saw for myself the same way I assumed I'd go to college, get a job, and then marry. Now, getting pregnant had come to seem like the core of my identity, the very reason I was put on this earth. I wasn't one of those girls who, growing up, had imagined myself in a white dress walking down the aisle. Nor had I fantasized about a baby straddling my hip. These had been abstract, far-off dreams, and I took for granted that they would naturally be realized when the time was right. And yet, as the prospect of a biological child threatened to slip through my fingers, I shocked myself with how firmly I tightened my grip. I had no idea how much I had wanted this.

So I sacrificed everything I could think to sacrifice and tried everything I could think to try. And still nothing happened. My body wouldn't budge. I was desperate for control. I felt *entitled* to control. Who was in charge of this body if not me? But for the first time in my life, no amount of will or effort could produce the outcome I wanted. My body had failed me. Though in the end, it felt as if I was the failure.

There was a quote I came across and couldn't seem to shake: *You don't have a soul. You are a soul. You have a body.* It was true. I understood it with as painful a clarity as I've ever understood anything.

After that first unsuccessful IVF we did another and another and then another. Four brutal rounds, six agonizing months.

It was time, finally, for a reckoning.

That reckoning came in the aftermath of our fourth round of IVF, when I found myself laying on a gurney in the ER, preparing to be sliced open so my surgeon could remove my right fallopian tube and the embryo that had implanted there. The doctor talked me through what was about to happen in the operating room—the incisions would be discreet, he explained, several centimeters etched below my bikini line. He cautioned that I would wake up feeling like I had been run over by a truck, but in a couple of weeks I should be good as new. As he spoke, I was far away. The skin belonged to me, the scars would be mine forever, but oddly, instead of feeling as if I was about to be invaded, I was preoccupied with how long the surgery would delay the start of our next cycle. My body had become an afterthought: Nothing more than the thing that I carried and that carried me.

"I can't believe I'm losing a fallopian tube," I finally said, disbelieving to be living this moment. "It's so," I grasped for the word. "Final." "Well, the truth is," he replied without hesitation, fixing his eyes on mine, "you don't need it anyway. You have true infertility. I don't believe you will ever be able to get pregnant without IVF."

And there it was: The Truth. In the two-and-a-half years of trying that had led to those words, throughout the many treatments and medications and procedures, as well as the countless consultations with and insights from all the professionals who had overseen my care, pinching and probing and stimulating and suppressing my body in a thousand different ways, no one, until now, had been willing or able to boil it down to The Truth. In that moment, my doctor assessed my fertility so acutely and with such clarity, I was left agape. *True Infertility*. It was a revelation, a scalpel to the heart.

Because despite the time that had passed, I had never considered myself infertile, though I realized I had long since met the clinical definition of trying unsuccessfully for one full year. I knew I wasn't getting pregnant, of course, that much was clear. And I had embraced the everyday realities of infertility. Indeed, I was immersed in its world, proficient in its language, discussing lab results and next steps with the ease of a med school graduate. I talked about and around it, referring, with comfortable distance, to my "experience with infertility" or my "issues with infertility." "We were thinking about going to Argentina this fall," I explained to a friend, revealing both everything and nothing, "but we've been dealing with some infertility stuff, so it didn't work out."

When I called my mom in the weeks leading up to our first round of IVF, two years into our experience, and shared our struggle with her for the first time, I avoided the "i" word entirely. After the usual nothings, I willed myself to begin.

"I wanted to let you know what's been going on with us," I paused briefly, then forced myself to keep going. "I think you know that Tim and I want to start a family, and we've been trying, but it hasn't been easy for us."

"Ooh. Ok, I'm sorry to hear that."

I had avoided sharing with my parents initially because I was uncomfortable discussing anything related to sex with my mom and dad. I figured I'd just wait and offer the good news once I was pregnant, a glossed-over, PG tale of conception. But as our journey got more complicated, I withheld the most significant thing happening in my life because bringing my parents into it would be an acknowledgment that this was a capital P Problem. I didn't need any well-meaning-yet-irritating questions, nor did I want to cause anyone worry. Once they knew it would officially be a Big Deal, though, of course, that had long since been the case.

"Yeah. They don't know what's wrong—why it hasn't happened yet—but it's been a really long road already," my words started coming out in a rush, each one running into the next. "I've been doing acupuncture, we tried a bunch of different medications, IUI—I mean it's been years of this. The next step is IVF, which we're starting at the end of the month."

"Oh, Amy," she said, though mostly she just listened, getting confirmation of what she surely had guessed at for some time. "We love you. It'll happen."

I was comfortable speaking of *infertility* when I needed to, but using the term *infertile* as a word to describe myself felt so weighted, final, almost a death sentence. Besides, I could readily tick off all the reasons why my being infertile didn't make sense; my still relative youth (now 33), the abundance of eggs that seemed to be practically spilling from my ovaries, the confidence of every medical professional who had treated me that somehow, this was just a glitch. *You've got plenty of time. You've got lots of eggs. You're so young. Everything looks great!* (Oh, really?! Then wtf is happening!!!) In my mind, I was always one acupuncture session or embryo transfer away from success. I *could* get pregnant; I just hadn't. Yet.

Now, my doctor was saying something different, something stark, something inarguably grim. *You have true infertility*, he told me, bluntly.

To 'have' something means you are host to a force—a virus, bacteria, genetics—governing your insides with a harsh, unforgiving rule. Infertility, though, seemed different. You have it, but the phrasing demands that you also must *be* it, part of the club for whom diagnosis is also a label: The Alcoholic. The Diabetic. The Schizophrenic. *I have infertility*, I could say, silently avoiding the more accurate, weightier label that years later I still can't say out loud: *I am infertile*.

That language insists upon ownership. There is no distance, no space to separate the thing you have from your truest self. The words wrapped themselves around me, the double helix of DNA descending down, the spiral encircling my center in a suffocating knot. If I were to accept that one declaratory sentence, all my frustration and answer-seeking and sacrifice would be rendered meaningless. Maybe it didn't matter that there was no diagnosis, no explanation, no family history, no hormone deficiency nor faulty reproductive organs to help make sense of it all. Maybe it didn't matter that there was no particular ailment to be blamed. I was afflicted, yes, but I must also be accountable.

Infertility was as much a part of me as my wide fingers, my sensitive nature, my compulsive need to be punctual. It was one of a million little aspects of me, none of which could be fixed or changed. They simply were.

I couldn't isolate a single decision I had made that could possibly have contributed to what I was experiencing. I fretted that the five-or-so years I'd spent on birth control had messed with my hormones, despite science insisting that's not a thing. So, it didn't feel true to say that anything was my fault. Instead, it was simply who I was. An infertile woman.

With that recognition, my perception shifted. My body could no longer be trusted. And though I still profoundly resented its refusal to do the one extraordinary thing it had been created to do, in the end, I realized that my resentment didn't matter. Wherever this mess was taking us, my body and I were in it together.

# Courage

***

My childhood bedroom is 32.4 miles from the Empire State Building, which sounds a lot closer than it is. It's located in a small suburb consisting of less than two square miles of land, a community too tiny to have a school bus system, too small to even qualify as a town. Officially, it is a village, named Pleasantville—of all things. New York City is close enough for class trips to Ellis Island and family outings to Knicks games, but my day-to-day—ice skating when the local pond froze over in winter, games of Marco Polo in the town pool in summer—more closely resembled a kid growing up outside Minneapolis, I'd imagine, than one raised in Manhattan.

***

When I moved into The City (capital T, capital C) for the first time, on January 1, it felt significant. It wasn't simply a new year or a new apartment I'd be inhabiting, but a new life entirely. Jessie, Tara, and I had grown up together in Pleasantville, and now, at 23 years old, we were moving on—together. We would be sharing 761 glorious square feet on the far, far Upper East Side, one block shy of East Harlem, crammed into a two-bedroom that we'd converted to three by having a temporary wall constructed in the center of the living room. We were firm believers that one woman's "cramped" is another woman's "cozy."

I remember that first night, the fatigue having set in after a day of unpacking and puzzling over the assembly instructions for IKEA furniture. It felt like we should be going out—it was a Saturday night in *New York City!*—but instead we stayed in our sweats, watching a movie I can't recall, taking stock of our new place. When the fake wall had gone up to siphon off a bedroom for Jessie, the living room had lost its windows. I remember how strange it appeared that first night; a shadowy box I wasn't yet familiar with, a diorama one of us might have constructed back in grade school, with three faceless figures arranged awkwardly inside. Without a portal to the outside world the living room had an ambiguity to it— as though you could lose your way in there, forget where you were.

A few steps away, in my bedroom, I took a moment to admire the set-up. I noted my bedding—flannel sheets in sage-green and a quilt with geometric shapes neatly arranged in their squares—which I'd removed from the packaging that very day. My bed was pushed up against the window, and my gaze drifted to the world beyond it; a row of adjacent rooftops, all dangling wires and smokestacks emitting puffs of grey into the cold air. I looked back at the quilt, then back at the smokestacks, and was struck by the discord. How homely my things read in here.

Crammed up near the bed was the piece I'd been most excited about: a wooden bookshelf I'd come across at the home décor shop in Pleasantville. It was tall, painted an oatmeal color, then gently rubbed, so as to appear aged. More than one person had pointed out I didn't have room for it, noting that shoving a clunky, unnecessary hunk of furniture into my shoebox of a room did not make much sense. But I could not be swayed to leave it behind. As a young magazine editor starting out in this hub of creativity, it felt symbolic. I was devoting space in my life to words, to books. Now, though, it became clear my quaint country bookshelf was out of place here; I only hoped the same couldn't be said about me.

\*\*\*

In those early days especially, the city required a piecing together: the connection of a never-ending series of dots. The physical neighborhoods were their own sort of puzzle: some areas easily placed through their names (Lower East Side, Upper West Side, Midtown), others revealing no geographic clues whatsoever (The Flower District, Hell's Kitchen, Alphabet City). Our neighborhood, full of 20-somethings newly out of college, was best known for its bars, which lined the avenues near our apartment, and where we began our immersion into city life.

We frequented them all—the sticky-floored one where we hurled ping pong balls into plastic cups of beer; the one with red velvet drapes and shelves of books that called to mind a scholarly library stocked with booze; the one with the pool table and pop-a-shot basketball machine that we loved for the free bags of chips and occasional carving station for anyone brave enough to trim off a sliver of communal turkey. We joked about the bar down the street called Blonde, Brunette, and a Redhead, because it could have been named for us—our little trio of roommates hustling to make it.

Jessie, the brunette, worked at a modeling agency, representing scores of beautiful people for on-camera jobs in commercials and TV. When she'd take calls, we'd smile at her serious-sounding negotiations about things like "the nudity clause" and "side boob." Tara, the redhead, bought commercial spots for Warner Bros. movies. She'd bring home DVDs of all the new TV pilots and was invited to movie screenings galore. And I was the blonde, working in magazines, where I got to meet and interview celebrities for a living, test beauty products, and write about fashion. Someone once referred to the three of us as having "sitcom jobs"—the fake-sounding work television roommates might do for a living. We laughed, but it was true; our jobs had an undeniable sparkle, exciting to talk about and full of perks.

The difference between our lives and those of our sitcom counterparts, however, was money. Somehow the TV versions of us would have had luxurious wardrobes and cushy furnishings, unencumbered by the very non-glamorous fiscal realities of being an underling in one of the most expensive cities in the world. When we signed our lease, our three salaries combined hadn't been enough to prove we could reliably pay the rent; a more accomplished adult had to co-sign for us. Our bank accounts were nearly empty, but we had a linen closet overflowing with Chanel mascara and designer shampoo I'd scored for free from the beauty closet at work.

Early on, Jessie, Tara, and I began referring to ourselves by our apartment number. Collectively, we were 7C. A group text might go out—*7C, what are we making for dinner tonight?*—pinging between three bedrooms, feet away from each other. Our friends adopted it too: *What's happening this weekend, 7C?* The term was efficient, but it also illuminated something deeper: we were a unit, in lockstep, sharing not only physical space but this pivotal moment in our lives. Three single women, navigating the city of our dreams, each of us striving for success in our careers and hoping to meet someone to fall in love with. We also intended to cram in a ton of fun along the way.

The pinnacle of that particular goal came one warm September night when our three paths, our three sitcom jobs, converged at the premiere party for *Gossip Girl*. The show, with its cast of bright young things, its promise of high fashion and higher drama set against the backdrop of the upper crust world of Manhattan private schools, had a ton of buzz, and the kickoff event was *the* place to be. Somehow, in this city full of people, all of 7C had scored an invite: Jessie, because one of the lead actresses was her client, Tara, because the show was produced by Warner Bros., and then me, a tag-along with my boss, the entertainment director of the magazine, who was attending to schmooze PR contacts and woo stars for covers and features. We were a world away from games of beer pong in the neighborhood.

My boss and I shared a cab from the office, and as we pulled up to Tenjune, the hotspot Meatpacking club where the party was being held, I gaped at the commotion out my window; flashing camera bulbs, stars posing hand-on-hip along the red-carpeted sidewalk. The event organizers found our names on the list and we squeezed our way inside, past men with chiseled jaws and paper-thin women, emerging into a space full of glamour and energy. I scanned the room for the only faces I would recognize, then grabbed my phone. *Where are you guys?* Jessie, Tara, and I texted our way to each other through the throng, and when we collided, little 7C in the center of this absurd and exhilarating scene, we traded hugs and disbelieving grins. Three girls from Pleasantville, lucky beyond words to be living it, even more so to be sharing it.

But it was what existed inside our four (mostly real) walls that truly sustained me, including our Sunday dinner ritual. During the week we'd scarf something cheap and easy—a frozen burrito, a cardboard tray of mac and cheese, cobbled-together English muffin pizzas. But come Sunday we'd divide the grocery list in thirds, hit up our neighborhood Gristedes, and pile into our miniature galley kitchen to cook ourselves a meal, chatting the whole way through. *When do you have that thing at work this week?* One of us might ask. Or we'd break down the headlines from the previous night out. *God, Jessie, who was that guy, he was hot! He for sure thought he was going to beat you in pool, it was very enjoyable to watch that play out.* Our food was nothing fancy; tacos were a standby, or cut-up chicken breasts sautéed in balsamic marinade. But we took pleasure in our meals, took pride in fumbling to pull them together in a kitchen of our very own. *Guys, this is a cooking show waiting to happen*, one of us said. *Yes! Oh my God totally, 20-somethings who have cheap frozen dinners all week and then cook one meal together on the weekend. When are we making our Food Network debut?* We named our imaginary hit "Sundays from Scratch."

When it was time to eat, we took the two steps into our living room, which offered no table and limited seating. We couldn't comfortably fit three-across on our butter-colored sofa, so two of us would take the couch and one would bring her plate to the floor, resting atop a comforter and a pile of pillows as we dined, the *60*

*Minutes* stopwatch ticking in the background. We practiced this ritual—sacred, un-missable—every Sunday for four years straight.

***

"So, who exactly is coming this weekend?" Tim asked from the driver's seat, his eyes fixed on the highway. "I can't remember—will 7C be there?" Many years had passed since our days in that apartment, but the label had stuck. Tim and I were en route to upstate New York; it was Labor Day weekend and we'd rented a house with a group of my childhood friends and their families. "Jessie's coming," I told him, "but Tara's not. And then it will be Kaitlyn, Katie, and Krissy, and all the husbands and kids." There were five small children among us at that point; Krissy and Katie both had two, Kaitlyn had one and was about to pop with her second, and Jessie was newly pregnant, barely starting to show. And then there was me, beginning treatment for my second IVF embryo transfer.

It never struck me as courageous to be going that weekend, though afterward I wondered if I should have opted out, to save myself from having to be around my pregnant friends and their babies. Perhaps. But it never occurred to me. Not even when Tara, who was still single, told me she was avoiding the whole thing. I didn't blame her, but somehow I had to believe our decades of history would make up for even the most glaring and painful differences in our present circumstances. My presence was a rejection of the idea that I, the non-mom, was somehow Other. I was there to prove to the group, to myself, that I still belonged. Was it going to be tricky at times, bordering on uncomfortable? Possibly. Could I handle it? Yes. I believed I could.

A day or two before the weekend, a group text popped up suggesting we celebrate Katie's birthday while we were all together upstate. I knew a great little bakery in Brooklyn, I replied, and could easily grab a cake. By early Friday evening, Tim was making the turn indicated by GPS into a driveway full of vehicles, most of them packed with car seats. That's when reality started to sink in. This was not one of our girls' dinners, a group around the table for a few hours drinking wine, trading hometown gossip, and catching up. This was entire families up close, in my face, for three days, and I was not going to be able to look away. My friends and their husbands had armloads of gear, of pack 'n' plays, of toys, of kids. Our hands were empty. I grabbed the cardboard bakery box, grateful to be showing up with something.

The rental house we all piled into was something of an oversized cabin, with plenty of bedrooms and a big backyard, but almost no natural light. Whether that was a product of few and small windows, or the fact that it rained the entire three days, I do not know. Tim and I, and Jessie and her husband, Chris, slept in the finished basement, the two rusty bedrooms adjacent to a wide open "party space," where the owners had arranged a long wooden bar, a pool table, and, oddly enough, a hot tub. It was a square, raised tub, the kind with a vinyl cover you have probably only ever seen on someone's deck. Only this was inside, in the far corner of the room, near a couch. As it turns out, hot bubbling water without sufficient ventilation creates a mildew-y film and foul dampness on everything within reach.

Being childless that weekend would have been painful no matter what. We were raw and vulnerable from years of struggle and a summer spent licking our wounds from our first failed round of IVF. But there is a world in which it could have been better. Had the sun shone, had we been able to do things—hike on a trail, sit by a lake—we might have been in a position to appreciate our unencumbered freedom. There were no naps to rush home for, no one to breastfeed or entertain or soothe down to sleep. Except the sun never appeared, so instead we were trapped in the shadowy cabin, bearing witness to what family life looked like for everyone else. The giggling kids to chase, the tears to dry and boo-boos to kiss, the uneaten chicken nuggets to toss, the endless questions to answer, the goodnight hugs to give, the loud and messy but undeniably warm and full and loving reality we wanted so badly.

Amidst the chaos of children, my friends and I tried to find moments for adult conversations. We all wanted to know how Kaitlyn and Jessie were feeling, if they had an inkling of whether their babies were boys or girls. I stood to the side of the kitchen listening, mindful to turn my lips up at the edges. Neither of them went into much detail or shared too excitedly, and I understood my presence to be the reason for it; there was a discomfort in talking freely about babies around me. Everyone also made sure to check in on how things were going with us; how was I doing, what was the latest with treatment. I appreciated being asked, but my answers never made it very far beyond top-line updates. I told them we were beginning a new cycle, a frozen embryo transfer this time, and that things had been hard but we were still hopeful. All of it factual, though none of it the real story. The truth of it—the desperation, the loneliness, the heartache—could scarcely be articulated, and certainly not offhandedly standing in a kitchen. Besides, if I got going, I might flood this rental with my tears, and I was not willing to be the reason we got charged for water damage.

Thinking back, I'm surprised by what I remember most from that weekend; what was vivid and urgent enough to calcify into memory. It wasn't Kaitlyn's basketball belly or glowing mama-to-be skin, or even the physical presence of five kids. I can't picture a single child's face in that house. Did I hold a baby? Chase a toddler? Did we hold off on eating dinner until the kids had gone to sleep? No clue. What stayed with me is Jessie at 12 weeks, her tummy barely the arc of a closed parenthesis, but whose presence—one of my closest friends with a baby growing inside—had a kind of voltage.

One day, for a few hours, the sky stopped spitting, and we all practically knocked each other over as we ran out of the house. The guys hit up a local golf course, the moms took the kids to a nearby park, and Jessie and I jumped in her car for a trip to the grocery store. She had always been the driver among our friends: As teenagers addicted to freedom, she would pick me up and we'd escape, meandering through neighboring towns, sometimes stopping on an especially quiet street where we'd swap places and she'd teach me, an unlicensed driver, the basics of signals and braking and parking. The summer of a harrowing breakup of mine in our 20s she drove us around the Jersey Shore, where we'd dramatically scream-sing the lyrics to Modest Mouse's "Float On" out our open windows. And now we were here, beside each other in the front seat once again. Unlike the cabin, or even this present moment in time, I knew how to exist in this space.

"How are you?" she asked, her voice acknowledging the depth of the question, and the likely truth of the answer. "I don't know," I replied, before following up with the truth. "Bad." Jessie had more insight into what was going on than the other girls, and she also had more insight into me. She could hear so much of what I didn't say. "How are *you*?" I asked in return. "How are you feeling?" They were all the same questions that had been posed already this weekend, but they sounded entirely different here in the car, just us. We traded more details, more complete pictures of our present selves, as candidly as compassion would allow. She, careful not to heighten my pain; I, mindful not to blunt her joy. We drove for a while, the grocery store was farther than we'd thought, all the roads unfamiliar, and it had the same aimless pleasure of when she'd pick me up in high school and we'd spend hours going nowhere.

***

Because I'd already begun eliminating toxins from my diet, I wasn't drinking that weekend, and never did touch the birthday cake, so I tended to turn in earlier than the rest of the group. Lying in bed, as the sound of meandering stories and raucous laughter seeped through the ceiling and the wall to the adjacent party room, my mind drifted ahead, to my upcoming embryo transfer, and back, to the last time we had been the lone childless couple, on a trip to Cape Cod with Tim's family just a few weeks earlier. It was a different trip, a different rental house, but the same story: We always seemed to be the puzzle piece that didn't quite fit.

One day in Cape Cod, most of the group left the beach early— Tim's sister, her husband, their toddler and brand-new baby, and his stepbrother, his wife, and their two tween boys. As our numbers dwindled, Tim's mom, sensing the quieter moment, had something to say. She wanted us to know how much she was praying for us, how deeply it pained her that we were struggling to start a family, that she recognized how difficult this time must be for us. I listened silently, nodding as she went on, book splayed in my lap, my eyes fixed on the ocean. *You two will make the absolute best parents,* she concluded. By then tears were gliding from behind my sunglasses.

There was no winning here, for us or our families. I didn't want to talk about our situation, but I also didn't want to *not* talk about it (simple enough, no?!). I wanted to be asked but I didn't know what to say. I was touched by Tim's mom's words, that she thought we would make great parents, but I was desperate to feel like I mattered, right in this moment, even if there was no baby on my breast or toddler on my hip, now or ever. It bothered me how we, the childless ones, were automatically assigned the couch to sleep on, though of course I understood why. It bothered me how it seemed we were all now supposed to refer to Tim's parents, and mine for that matter, by their grandparent names, titles I couldn't bring myself to use given we had no children of our own. It bothered me that to the parents in the group, we were simply along for the ride, eminently flexible and beholden to the whims of other people's children, like the night we went to dinner at 5 p.m. and had to leave abruptly mid-meal, plates still full of food, because one of the kids was fussy and unhappy enough to require an emergency exit. I wanted to finish my fried seafood, dammit, and my half-empty (half-full?!) beer. But mostly I didn't want to feel the particular ache that comes with invisibility.

On the night we abandoned our meal at the restaurant, I followed everyone out, Tim and I heading straight to our car, while the rest of his family gathered around the rain-slickered fishermen figures on the grass. They were the kind with the cutout faces, and we watched as three generations took turns sticking their heads and arms through the holes, snapping pictures and laughing at the silliness of each person's transformation. We were quiet, waiting in the parking lot until they were done, and then we all drove home.

Courage, it seems, can have many different textures. It isn't always big and bold, the pounding heart, the electrified senses. Sometimes it is quiet grit in the face of the familiar, a soft smile at someone else's joy, even when you so badly want what they have. It's a lump in the throat; a swallow; a straightening of the spine; a willingness to stand on the floor in the morning and rise out of bed, forcing one foot in front of the other. All of it unglamorous, unseen. The fortitude of simply showing up. Of bearing witness. Of not averting your eyes.

***

We awoke the Monday of Labor Day weekend to sparkling sunshine, but man—it was time to go. Jessie was in her sweats making breakfast, and we got to talking in the kitchen, as we had so many millions of mornings back in 7C. This time the topic was decaffeinated coffee (depressing in its own specific way), which, on account of her pregnancy and my aspiring-pregnancy, we had both taken to drinking. Jessie was explaining how she'd learned coffee is often surprisingly full of pesticides, how pods specifically tend to be laden with chemicals, but that she'd found one particular brand of beans that were clean and delicious. "I literally had no idea," I said, mentally tabulating how much toxic coffee I'd been chugging, registering how uninformed I was, how inadequate my dietary restrictions had been, and imagining that if I switched to Jessie's brand, if I eliminated just one more thing, then maybe I, too, might be lucky enough to get pregnant. "Will you email me the name of the one you like?" Everyone was packing up and saying goodbye, and one of the girls asked to see Jessie's belly, so she bashfully lifted her t-shirt a tiny bit. I winced and watched.

Tim and I were in the car on the country roads leading away from the cabin for a while before one of us broke the silence. "Are you ok?" A pause. "I'm ok. How are you?" As we got closer to the city, which held the promise of appointments and procedures, leading us farther away from the out-of-sorts summer that was, we finally found things to laugh about. How the weekend hadn't been bad so much as comically terrible. And that musty smell! I pulled the neck of my shirt up to my nose; it was still with us in the car, it was following us home.

After 72 hours amid the cacophony of small children, our apartment seemed especially empty. But it felt good to be there. We had showed up, and now we were home, back in the one place I could cry or collapse or scream or sleep or shower or slam or rant it all away, so that I might be courageous enough to try again tomorrow. I loved that apartment. All it needed was the third roommate we'd been searching for.

# Disappointment

This is how my fantasy went: Alone in our apartment as morning sunshine hit hardwood, I would rest on the couch until the moment of readiness, when nerve outweighs fear, when the swell of inertia was enough to pull me up, weight distributed evenly across both feet, and lead me into the bathroom to pee on a stick. As I dreamt it there was no lapsed time, no incubation period for the urine to seep through the absorbent strip; the results were instantaneous, because today I was not merely, ordinarily, pregnant, but overwhelmingly so. When the plus sign or the double pink lines or the bold word PREGNANT appeared, unmistakable, I would drop down onto the lid of the toilet, or maybe the side of the tub, covering my mouth with one palm, gripping the test with the other. In jubilant disbelief I would shake my head soundlessly, beaming, eyes locked on that white plastic stick.

Eventually, I would pick myself up and float through the day. I would not call my mom, or text a friend, or blurt it out to the woman who made my latte every morning at Starbucks. For those hours, the fact of our baby would exist inside me and nowhere else. Before words were assigned to him, before the truth of her was uttered aloud, released into the air as one more fleck of knowledge swirling around the universe, the news would remain deep within me, in its purest form. That moment, after the thing is known but before it is shared, would be sacred, unforgettable, and totally mine.

That was how my fantasy started, the pregnancy itself as point of entry, the *knowing*. But after the knowing was the telling, and that was the part I came to fixate on.

The thought of telling Tim exhilarated me, stoking my unspoken joy until I could rush home from work and wait for him to arrive. Reclining on the couch, waiting in a silent, still apartment, eyes fixed toward the front door, listening for the twist of his key in the lock. When he walked in, I would look at him, me knowing, him not, and I would observe him in the waning moments of his life Before. I would be calm, revealing nothing, and we would greet each other, chitchat about our days at work, debate what to have for dinner. And then at some point, my heart would take flight, a flush of anticipation seeping across my cheeks. My tone would change. I wouldn't say much, the exact words weren't the point. The announcement would be simple and quiet, maybe something like, "I have something to tell you." At which point Tim would look up and I would pause. "You're going to be a dad."

That was it. I would watch as his face changed, neurons firing, emotions igniting. His eyes would soften, brighten, glisten. His mouth would stretch into a stunned smile. We would embrace, exclaim, shake our heads in shock, reflexively move but not know where to go. We would talk and talk, clinging to the precise coordinates of that beautiful, perfect moment for as long as possible. The moment that separated life Before from life After.

This pregnancy fantasy occupied my consciousness for months, curving my lips into a smile while riding the subway, waiting in line for that latte, washing my hair. I couldn't quite place the tactile details of our future child—the arc of her glistening cheeks grinning up from the bath; the weight and warmth of his tiny body curled against my chest. So I let my mind dwell on what it could make sense of: Tim and me, happy news, a beginning.

The role this fantasy put me in—the knower, the teller—was another dimension of its allure. I had never had the opportunity to share something so meaningful. To change someone's life. Reproductively speaking, it's a position of advantage, one in which we women don't often find ourselves. Instead, we endure decades of inconvenient periods, find ourselves saddled with the burden of birth control since men would really prefer not to wear condoms. We are biologically tasked with the planning and responsibilities that accompany our anatomy, but now, finally I was being shown the power that came with it, a gift. *The* principal, primal gift of being a woman. This body I was born into would afford me a transformative power: to bear a child, to grow it within my body, to deliver it into the wild world. And it all began with telling my husband he was going to be a dad. Imagining myself as the architect of a moment so much bigger than both Tim and me took my breath away.

The trouble is, my daydream hinged on the approximations that accompany natural conception. When I *might* be ovulating fed into when we *might* have conceived, which led to the mystery of when I *might* be able to test. Once we began synthetically triggering my egg's release, there was scientific certainty to the process. The guesswork, and the potential to surprise Tim, was gone.

Indeed, I now had the duty, a duty that fought against my most fervent beliefs about how getting pregnant should go, to report the result of every test, every step of the way. It felt like an intrusion, a loss of my fundamental right as a woman to learn I was pregnant on my own terms, at a time of my choosing, all by myself. It was our news ultimately, but it felt like it needed to be my news first. Now, it wouldn't be.

Once or maybe twice, with righteousness and indignation ringing in my ears, I made an independent decision to test, before our decided-on date. *It's my body, I can test whenever I want to,* I justified to myself. *Who could possibly argue that I'm not entitled to that?* So, I did. And then I waited on the couch for Tim to get home from work in a scene that looked very much like my fantasy—down to the quiet click of his key in the door—only this was that scene's mirror image: everything was on the wrong side.

"It's a no," I declared bluntly, moments after we'd said hello, as Tim was still crossing the room toward me.

"What's a no?" It took him a moment to orient himself, his face scanning mine for clues.

"I tested. It's a no."

"Wait, what? You tested?" He had stopped moving. "I thought we couldn't find out until Wednesday?" His face had fallen. "Are you sure?"

We were deep enough into the experience by then for testing to be fraught, my taking it into my own hands almost felt dangerous. So many powerful emotions on the line, both of us scarred by all the disappointments, and here, I had deepened Tim's pain by not letting him brace for another.

His face hardened first, then his tone. "You can't just fucking hit me with that when I walk in the door." I avoided his eyes. "I get that it's your body, but this is about both of us. I have a right to know what's going on."

I instinctively recoiled, defensive, but I also knew that I had been careless and blunt in my delivery. It wasn't fair of me to surprise him like that, but at the same time, none of this was fair. I was grasping for control of something—anything—and maybe testing was the only scenario in which I could be in charge.

That night, after more discussion, we agreed that from then on, Tim could be home for the testing. He wanted to be present so that he might be prepared. How could I blame him? I never did explain that I had a fantasy about how it would go, that it really mattered to me that I find out by myself. I guess it seemed too silly to put into words. Given our experience, it would be foolish to hope for anything more than the news itself.

But as the nos continued to pile up, Tim proposed a new protocol. "What if I go into the bathroom to check the test?" he offered, "instead of you. Or what if we both go in together?" I was familiar with this kind of logic, since I practiced it myself. It was based on the magical thinking we had both gradually adopted; that perhaps if we went about this differently, the outcome would be different. A fresh pair of eyeballs could have the power to both read the test and somehow change the test. But as much as I believed in Tim's strategy, I couldn't shake my conviction as to how the process should play out. What if the next time was actually it? I still wanted to be the first to know and the one to tell Tim. It has to be me, I told him, unwavering in my fealty to this innermost fantasy.

Soon enough, though, I stopped testing at home altogether. It had become too torturous to feel the swell of anticipation, to experience the heart-soar of possibility in those few agonizing minutes, the held-breath, the stopped-time, while my urine seeped through the stick. When the negative result appeared, as it did, every single time, my spirit was crushed just a little bit more. The damage was starting to feel irreparable. Besides, once we were doing IVF, I trusted that the fertility clinic was performing their blood test, more sensitive than a home urine test anyway, at the earliest possible date of detection. And until the results came in, I could still believe. I had reached the point where I needed to hope more than I needed to know.

***

Eventually, I came to understand that surprising Tim was not going to be possible. I would never have those few, cherished hours with the knowledge of our baby living inside me, twinkling beneath my flesh. Now, a stranger would know before I did, and would share the news, if ever there was news to tell. I experienced far deeper, more tangible disappointments along the way; the failed cycles, the plans canceled, the mourning that my mom and dad would be denied the gift of grandparenting my child. There were so many losses, but this was one I never spoke of, not even to Tim. This one was all mine.

# *Patience*

To be patient: withstanding calmly, quietly persevering

To be a patient: one who is under medical care

Both definitions, the adjective and the noun, derived from the Latin word *patiens*, one who suffers, are essential to the experience of infertility.

To be patient is to suffer through idleness—the pain is inflicted when the mind is left to gnaw on itself. To be a patient is to suffer at the whim or misfortune of the body. To be a patient patient is to experience infertility.

Waiting, in many ways, *is* infertility. It is required even before the diagnosis, when infertility is still only one possibility, in the "hopefully that's not what we're dealing with" stage, as you tick through the required 12 months of trying (if you happen to be under 35) or six months (if you're over 35). You must wait to find out if you are infertile, and you must wait for everything else once you do.

The good kind of waiting, which is of course not good at all, but is in fact terrible and simply happens to be more easily tolerated, is the everyday waiting of an IVF cycle. Waiting for doctor's appointments, to hear your name called in the waiting room, for the phone to ring with medication instructions, for a partner to get home to administer injections. Waiting up for a late-night trigger shot, for the egg retrieval, for the news of how many eggs fertilized, then for a call with news of how many made it to a more advanced stage of development. Waiting for the transfer, then, possibly, for the number of additional embryos that have passed the rigors of genetic testing. Waiting to see a therapist in part to cope with all the waiting. And, finally, waiting for the call with pregnancy test results, which ironically, is often not the final call at all. After that, there's more waiting—for a chemical pregnancy to fizzle and die out, for an ectopic pregnancy to reveal itself, for surgery after that. Improbably, each one of those were the easier waits, I found, because they were separated from each other by moments of action, and because they could for the most part be endured with hope; to be trying to get pregnant, actively, was to have a chance to make it so.

The lapses between cycles, on the other hand, when we were not actively trying, introduced me to the depths of my suffering. That idleness was more trying than sticking needles through my flesh, than hearing so many friends announce their pregnancies, than having dye shot around my cervix or a nub of my uterus snipped off for a biopsy, than my fear of the unknown, than my skin being pulled open for surgery, than my escalating loneliness. It was more trying even than getting end-of-cycle calls from nurses saying they were so sorry, but—. When we weren't trying there was no hope of anything working. That kind of waiting felt like failing in the most passive, lethargic, hopeless way, and we endured it again and again—when the embryology lab closed for routine upkeep for a month. When there's nothing to be done until your period comes—another six weeks down the drain. Once I had a grip on the timeline, if I received news of another delay, my reactions were nothing short of ferocious; scream-sobs, hyperventilating breaths, blotchy hive-rashes. After one IVF cycle I wrote an email to a friend explaining how, in order to kill some lingering cells from an otherwise extinguished pregnancy, I might have to take a drug, methotrexate, whose potency is such that it's also used to destroy cancer cells in chemotherapy patients. To allow the drug time to retreat from my bloodstream, we wouldn't be able to try again for three months:

*If that is the case, I feel like I will die. I can't explain it, but it is an outcome that makes me unable to breathe. I had an extreme physical reaction after talking to [our doctor], in all of the mess that this entire situation has been, this is my trigger. Nothing affects me the way the prospect or reality of waiting does.*

To read it back now, *I feel like I will die*, when the sensory truth of that sentiment is long gone, its grooves and creases no longer familiar, my instinct is to be embarrassed at the note of melodrama, as though I was 15 and the boy I liked didn't like me back. Except I wasn't 15. I was 33, facing down three months without hope and the life-sustaining oxygen it provided, and I meant it. I felt that I could not continue on as me, in my body, living my life, waiting three more months to try again. Maybe I would slowly extinguish, dimming to the moment of eventual darkness, or maybe I would spontaneously dissolve into a mass of tiny particles, my patience tested to the point of oblivion.

When I was busy waiting for periods, for answers, for a miracle, I was also waiting to live.

\*\*\*

The waits weren't always agonizing, not at first. There was no single moment, no shift, when the patience required of me became too much to bear. I believe my despair in waiting was a product of accumulation, the days turning to weeks, the months disappearing into years.

Early on, just three months after I had gone off birth control, I was optimistic (delusional?) enough to believe that I could control things, that I would perhaps get pregnant when it was convenient for me. Wouldn't that be nice, I plotted, I'll plan it all out so as not to trouble myself with less-than-ideal timing (*bahaha*). I remember that Tim and I were scheduled to go on a wine tour in October, his Christmas gift to me, and with what now feels like hubris, I dared to hope that I would not be pregnant when the time for tasting and sightseeing with friends arrived. "That would obviously stink if you were pregnant," Tim admitted, when I fretted to him about the timing. "But then you'll be happy to be pregnant and you'll have fun with your friends no matter what." I crossed my fingers, uncertain which way it would go or what I hoped for.

When the day came, a warm, sun-soaked Saturday morning, Tim and I and four of our friends tucked into our chariot for the day. We talked and laughed and sipped coffee, making our way from Lower Manhattan to the North Fork of Long Island, where the grays of our everyday landscape gave way to the palette of early autumn. We whizzed past farms and wound our way down tree-lined drives, the leaves clinging to their greens despite being slowly dip-dyed red and yellow.

I was relieved—joyful even—not to be pregnant that day. None of us had kids, so there was no one to rush home to, no familial responsibilities to distract us. We were aligned in our goals, which were less about the appreciation of wine than the explicit consumption of it. Our stated mission: No Wine Left Behind! The tour took us to three vineyards, and there were more pours than I could count. Dense, round purples, cloying pinks, tart whites. Bottle after bottle, taste after taste. Surely we ate that day, though I cannot recall taking a single bite of food. The sun sizzled high and hot in the afternoon, making the dusty air waver and the buzz of wine headier, more persuasive.

At the vineyards, our drunkenness wasn't noteworthy. Our laughter, increasingly loud and raucous, was muted by the breeze and surrounding vines. In line for the bathroom, we bumped up against bachelorette parties, and beside their sashes and coordinating t-shirts, we appeared composed, collected. So, it wasn't until we returned to the city that the mess of us was revealed. We wobbled into our apartment building, arms awkwardly clutching the bottles of wine we had collected. It was in the elevator that one of those bottles slipped, crashing to the floor in a million shards of glass and a wide purple puddle.

It both registered and didn't. We cared and didn't. "Whoooops!" "Ohhhh, shit!" "That suuuuucks." We giggled guiltily. We entered the apartment and guzzled water. I grabbed my computer and showed the group an *American Idol* performance I'd been talking up all day ("We've Got Tonite" sung by Phillip Phillips—it's very much worth a Google). Finally, we stumbled back outside for fried chicken, which we gnawed until teeth hit bone. My head buzzed, my eyes blurred. We said goodnight.

I awoke Sunday cloaked in drunk-shame. *The mess in the elevator,* my head throbbed. My thoughts turned to Harvey, our curmudgeonly doorman. He was a legendary character around the building who could often be found reading the New York City tabloids, complained endearingly about almost everything, and relished the opportunity to give the same deadpan response any time we asked if he'd like a cup of coffee when we were running out: "as long as it's not from Starbucks." I thought of Harvey knowing we were the source of the broken glass and pool of wine on the elevator floor. We hadn't acknowledged it or apologized. Someone else had to clean up our mess, and knowing it had all unfolded in broad daylight heightened the ugliness. I had been relieved not to be pregnant that day, to carouse freely, sing loudly, drink excessively with my friends. And the morning after, I was relieved that these days of irresponsibility were nearly behind me.

And yet—the party continued. Months later Tim and I found ourselves on a whirlwind weekend in Miami that Desi and I had rushed to get on the books before I was pregnant. It was the latest— and, I hoped, last—stop on what had come to feel like a goodbye tour. Goodbye to booze, goodbye to splurgy spending, goodbye to a carefree life. In the early days of waiting to get pregnant, I expressed—exulted in—my freedom. Freedom to drink, to travel, to continue on as I had for the past decade, only with the added benefit of an awareness that these days were numbered. I was free and had an appreciation of that freedom; each plan existing as a tentative, hypothetical until I woke up, still not pregnant, and determined I could in fact do that One Last Thing.

My patience had a rosy cast in those days, plumped up with eagerness, the shiny sort that's only possible when you know the thing you're waiting for is surely on its way. When it's only a matter of time. It all amounts to a sort of ease—wait with a friend, a drink, bathed in sunshine. *Enjoy it while you can!* I wasn't pregnant in Miami—at least, I didn't think I was. Because my period was erratic and unpredictable, I often walked around convinced there was a baby starting to grow in there, so I sipped each of my ten thousand cocktails that weekend with an anticipatory guilt. *What if this is really it?*

Before dawn on the morning of our flight back to New York an iPhone alarm cut through the utter blackness of the room. As I placed my feet on the floor beside the bed, a sensation of achy wetness roused my senses. My lower half was covered in blood. My period had arrived. Vacation was over.

\*\*\*

When I gave notice at work after learning of our first IVF failure, I didn't fully grasp that in doing so, I was allowing for a sort of perpetual continuity between the stagnation of my insides and the newly hollowed-out world beyond. I went from having an unproductive body to being an unproductive person.

It wasn't that I reclined into laziness; on the contrary, I pursued productivity vigorously, within the limited realm to which I had confined myself. I busied my mind, researching information on Polycystic Ovary Syndrome with the dedication of a scholar, devouring essays on the infertility site Resolve.org and blog posts written by women struggling to conceive. I filled up my appointment calendar, hustling to the acupuncture and therapy visits that helped tether my weightless weeks to the ground. I busied my hands; cooking wholesome soups and nourishing grains to purify my insides and counteract all the synthetic agents being syringed through my skin. I busied my soul; trying hot yoga as a way to draw my painful emotions up and out, making their way to the surface through my pores, my sweat, my tears. I was trying, in a way, to mimic my previous life, when I had spent mornings jostling up against the hordes of commuters on the rush hour subway, waiting for coffee in a line of caffeine-starved New Yorkers, bustling down the sidewalk and into work, where I attended meetings, conducted interviews, edited stories, after which I might exercise, or meet a friend for dinner. Those hours, those days had been full. Now I was merely fabricating action, the only antidote I knew to waiting. And there was no baby to show for any of it.

It was a supreme privilege to be able to forgo my paycheck and commit myself to the process of trying to get pregnant. I'd like to say I did something noteworthy during that three-year vacuum of space and time in which I waited. Read the classics or joined a political campaign or converted my rudimentary Spanish to fluency. I began the process of becoming a volunteer through a local service group, stopping short of actually leaving the house to attend orientation. When the moment came to engage with the outside world, to step beyond the bounds of my private fertility bunker, even for an hour, I couldn't do it. My insistence toward productivity, toward purpose, was outmatched only by my allegiance to the cause. To focus my attention elsewhere would be healthy, I recognized, but also somehow an abandonment of my commitment. Proof that I wasn't all-in. I was overwhelmed by the need to act, to do, to counteract the stillness of infertility—but I also couldn't let myself escape it.

Instead, I jumped into a most convenient black hole of false productivity: Google. I compulsively Googled everything I was feeling, anything that occurred to me, really, fixating on any hair-splitting nuance that might divide one sensation from another. Every symptom I decidedly felt, every absent symptom I didn't, and what if any significance there was to experience or not experience such a thing at whatever precise phase of a cycle I happened to be in. *Is implantation spotting common? But, like, how common? Slight cramping pregnancy symptom?* I excavated hyper-specific corners among the thousands of pregnancy chat rooms, unearthing long-dormant conversations from five and nine and twelve years prior, inviting myself to eavesdrop, learning from these women's most personal experiences, about the children they had and those they were wishing for, their miscarriages, their failed cycles, their faith, their sex lives, and of course, their possible pregnancy symptoms. The latter I read with obsessive interest, scrutinizing them against my observations of my own body, squinting to see whether I was feeling what they had felt, and what if anything that could tell me about the single question around which my existence orbited: was I pregnant? *Sore breasts early pregnancy? Small amount of discharge could I be pregnant?*

I'd scroll through pages of comments, following each thread to its conclusion, because I was desperate to stay in the company of these strangers; my new friends. I learned to speak their pregnancy shorthand, which I found embarrassingly hokey yet quickly adopted and incorporated into my searches: DH for dear husband, AF for Aunt Flo, meaning your period; the less charming CM for cervical mucus. Then there was TWW, the two-week wait between ovulation and the moment of truth, and BFP for a big fat positive pregnancy test (BFN was its unfortunate opposite). The generous thing to do was to wish the other women Baby Dust—a magical chat room vapor of luck, hope, and possibility.

All the while I remained voiceless, invisible, lurking. Not an internet troll of course, maybe something more akin to a gnome? If there is such a thing? A friendly, albeit quiet, visitor. I frequented chat rooms but did not chat. I did not pose a question, form a friendship, or connect with one single soul. When I was on my goodbye tour, I had done my waiting in the company of friends, laughing, drinking, and traveling. If those waits were a celebration of my freedom, these were defined by my confinement, my only companion the vague outline of my reflection projected on the screen of my computer atop the words of strangers.

Part of me wishes I could see a record of my Google search history, which must exist in some cloud somewhere. Part of me is also deeply grateful that I can't, given it might look a *tad* obsessive. Those searches were the most accurate reflection of every nagging fear and optimistic moment and innocuous sensation I felt, a post-internet portrait of desperation.

Tim was aware of my searches, occasionally reading over my shoulder. "So, basically, cramps can mean you're getting your period or you're pregnant? And a headache can mean you're getting your period or you're pregnant?" He'd smile, sounding dubious, while I would actively ignore him and his valid-yet-unhelpful points. He was particularly amused by the chat room lingo, which he liked to use to break the ice in tense moments, of which there were many. The morning of a retrieval or transfer, or the hours before we were expecting the nurse's call with pregnancy test results, he would lean over and smile, whispering into my ear the most powerful sentiment one could offer: "I wish you...*baby dust!*"

Still, I was careful not to let him see the extent of my searching. If he came home from work while I was in the midst of my hard-hitting "research," I would snap my laptop shut. But he could usually guess what I had been up to. "Please put your computer away," there was a plaintive note in his voice. "It's a waste of time, you can't trust what anyone is saying there anyway. Why are you doing this to yourself?" He understood the way the searches fed my hope, or despair, infesting my mind either way. But what he didn't understand was how they occupied my consciousness in a way it needed to be occupied, allowing me to think about and engage with the only topic that mattered to me. These pseudo answers, these wholly unscientific case studies, flimsy as they may have been, gave me a sense of control over something that was entirely out of my hands.

During the in-between times, especially, when it was too soon to pee on a stick, too soon for a blood pregnancy test, I used search terms to try to glean an understanding of whether whatever method we were using—IVF, IUI, Clomid, regular old sex—had worked. If I could come to a conclusion sooner and reduce that interminable wait time by days or even hours, my research would be worth it.

Those Google searches were the crutch propping up my patience, but while I was keeping myself busy, approximating productivity to fill the waiting, time—days, weeks, months—disappeared, the calendar year rendered meaningless. It could be summer or winter, April or October. It didn't matter because we were never any "closer." We were either at zero or 100; there was no in-between.

The only concept of time that registered in my brain was the progression of other women's pregnancies. Fertility was the sun around which my world orbited. I told time by gestation. A friend delivering her baby was my alert that almost nine months had passed since her pregnancy announcement, which still felt fresh in my mind. An acquaintance who had recommended a book when we'd both been trying had since gotten pregnant, carried to term, given birth and was now celebrating an infant's first birthday. That was nearly two years gone by—the familial milestones of other lives punctuating the emptiness of my own.

As for me, what did I have to show for those 9 months, 12 months, 18 months, 24 months, 36 months? Patience. I was both overloaded and running out.

# Uncertainty

***

Every morning, I opened my eyes and wondered if my period had arrived overnight, if the sheets would be soaked beneath me. When I got out of bed and walked into the bathroom, I'd peer between my thighs to see if I'd find a few drops of red disrupting the homeostasis of the toilet bowl. Or perhaps it would show up later that day. I never knew what to expect.

Irregular periods are where it all began for me. For my entire menstruating life, beginning in middle school all the way through the five years in my late 20s that I spent on birth control, my cycle had been predictable. But then I went off the NuvaRing the month Tim and I started trying to have a baby, and everything changed. My cycle length extended: First by a few days, then more alarmingly to 44 days, 56 days. I'd wait five weeks, six weeks, seven weeks for a period. When it did come there was the initial crush of disappointment, followed by frenzied excitement. Forward movement! Now the appointments, action, plans could resume, with a renewed sense of promise. When there was no period life stood still. All my hopes and dreams were carbon copied and pinned on tomorrow. Again, and again.

One Thanksgiving we holed up in our apartment waiting for my period instead of spending the holiday with Tim's family in Florida. If it arrived, we would need to go into the clinic the following morning to start a fresh round of IVF, though no one could be sure when it would show up. We might need to be at home, we might not. It was clear to me that whatever good the Florida sunshine would have done for my psyche was not worth the risk of jeopardizing our chance to start a new cycle. So we hunkered down in New York, went to Chinatown for soup dumplings, held our breath through the last few episodes of *Breaking Bad*. I waited for the toilet water to turn red. It didn't.

Whenever my period did arrive one question was answered while a million more arose, as Tim and I played out parallel scenarios, arranging our worlds around the details of every potential reality. *If we wind up retrieving the eggs next Tuesday, and if we do a five-day transfer instead of a three, then we'll definitely be able to make it to so-and-so's birthday party. But if the stimulation goes an extra couple of days and we don't do the retrieval until the 12th, then we'll have to cancel that weekend at the beach. On the other hand, if we hold off an extra day and transfer on Thursday instead of Wednesday, then that would push the pregnancy test until Saturday, which means we wouldn't get results until Monday; do we really want to deal with 48 extra hours of waiting?* My brain craved order, lunging for certainties when they arose, so that I might orient myself within the exasperating realm in which I found myself. Each set of facts and resultant decision led to an intricate web of possibilities, a network of silky threads promising symmetry and order. But a single nick in a single strand and it all collapsed in on itself.

Estrogen levels, follicle diameters, the workmanship of my left ovary versus my right—I could explain all of it, citing test results, ultrasounds, and regular blood work as evidence. I had enough stats on my own biology to fill a textbook, but somehow, I had never been less certain of what was actually going on inside my body. I was weighed down with facts, but my entire existence was hypothetical. Still, I had faith in the experts. A privilege I've long benefited from but rarely appreciated is that when a doctor strides into my examining room with a *so what do we have going on here today,* I am seen. Listened to. Treated with dignity and humanity. Part of the inheritance handed to me as a white American has been an implicit trust in the medical system. I haven't valued it nearly enough.

As stated in my medical chart:

## HISTORY OF PRESENT ILLNESS:

33 yo G1P0 TTC x 2.5 years. H/o ? PCOS with 34-56-day cycles. Exercises 4 days per week with barre classes and running. AMH was 2.58 in 9/2013. Underwent 4 cycles of clomid at [ob/gyn], one with IUI without success. Normal SA initially, subsequent samples with high volume and borderline normal concentration. HSG at [first clinic] showed normal cavity and likely patent tubes (R obscured by venous intravasation of dye). At that time was told to try letrozole IUIx2. Subsequently did IVF at [first clinic], FSH at 200 units, triggered at 18mm with E2 of 2863, 19 mature eggs, 12 fert, 1 blast transferred with aggressive luteal support. Subsequently had FET of 1 embryo and then another FET with 2 blasts (September and October). October FET resulted in biochemical pregnancy. Still has 3 blasts frozen. Was told to do IVF with PGS.

Thirty-three years old, trying to conceive for two-and-a-half years. I was switching to a new fertility clinic, and my doctor's summary at our initial appointment listed numbers, details and acronyms that told the story of my treatment in a succinct paragraph that would have been indecipherable to the uninitiated. Included in my medical chart from that day is an official Assessment, a stock form of labels and corresponding boxes meant to help identify all factors related to a patient's infertility. *Tubal factor. Unilateral obstruction. Bilateral obstruction. Adhesions. Hydrosalpinx.* None of those applied. *Uterine anomalies. Septate. Bicornuate. Unicornuate. Cavitary adhesions. Other.* Again, nothing. The list went on. *Recurrent abortions. Ovarian cyst. Fibroid uterus. Uterine polyps.* 80 boxes. 80 potential explanations. Zero checks.

The only mark on the page is next to *Primary infertility*: The problem acknowledged, the cause left blank. To see dozens of unchecked boxes is to feel relief, in a sense, because at face value the Assessment has determined that nothing is wrong. Except, of course, everything was wrong.

Even after that form was completed, after the additional testing and all the future empirical data was collected, the ultimate judgment on me was: we don't know. Not *We don't know, **yet***. Rather: *We don't know, period*. Case closed. My official diagnosis: Unexplained infertility. Medically, that explanation is legitimate. As a patient, it feels remarkably, unacceptably, incomplete. A radical void.

In truth, it's a mystery, one more personal and consequential than all the others I've been drawn to since childhood. Games of "Clue" and Sunday night episodes of *Murder, She Wrote*. So many decades spent swept up in the crime, hungry for the solve, collecting clues as information is deliberately revealed and withheld, engaging in a piecing together that teases and toys with my brain until a picture forms and I'm rewarded with the ultimate satisfaction: an answer. In the end, as far as I've ever known, there is always an answer.

And I've long fancied myself just the one to find it. See, if I possess any sort of superpower, it is vigilance, well-practiced since I was small. I may not have been able to prevent the runaway train that is diabetic shock, but if I paid close enough attention, observed the most inconspicuous details of what was happening around me— has he eaten yet? Is it too hot outside? Is he starting to mumble?— then perhaps I could anticipate it. I could be prepared. The person in charge might lose control, but not me. I would not lose control.

The Curious Case of my Infertility, as far as I was concerned, was a mystery just like any other. Besides, medicine was supposed to be a world of certainty and science, facts and truth. The experts in the field have the astonishing power to inform a patient of the eye color assigned to a future human when it is nothing more than a collection of cells in a test tube. But now, those same experts could not say what was going on inside the body of the fully formed human right in front of them. And if the obstacle couldn't be named, it seemed unlikely that I could ever be successful against it.

I first heard the term *PCOS* from a doctor in my OB/GYN practice about a year after Tim and I started trying. There was a desk drowning in books and papers between us, and as I listened to her calmly and warmly explain that I had high ovarian reserve and weak ovulation, I jotted words in my notebook, an investigator through and through. *Resistant to ovulation. No dominant follicle. Clomid – take days 5-9 – creates stronger egg.* I remember hearing her say something about PCOS, though interestingly I didn't write it down. Her reference must have been casual, noncommittal, but to someone desperate for an explanation, my mind heard it and held on. *A clue.* When I typed it into Google later, I learned that PCOS—Polycystic Ovary Syndrome—is a hormonal imbalance marked by irregular cycles, weight gain, excessive hair growth, and infertility. Hmm. It wasn't exactly right (I had two symptoms out of four), but I could try it on, make it fit.

Five months later I found myself in the office of a reproductive endocrinologist. I had been promoted to The Big Leagues. When he made an offhanded reference to PCOS, I interjected. "What does that mean," I asked, frustrated that no one was being direct. "My OB/GYN brought up PCOS too, but she didn't actually say I have it. Do I have it?" He leaned back with an I-know-everything smile, nodding; he'd been expecting my question. "Patients always want clarity," he said, his hands clasping, then parting so they could assist in making his point. "They want to hear 'yes, you have this' or 'no, you don't. But in reality, these diagnoses exist in shades of grey. Do I think you have PCOS? No. But you probably fall somewhere on the spectrum."

In the moment, his answer satisfied me. As our relationship continued, however, I found less comfort in my doctor's words. In the seven months I spent under his care he never bothered to learn my name. To be fair, I rarely saw him. Instead, I felt like a blurred-out face arriving every morning, an anonymous infertile woman signing in on a screen, not even getting to exchange a smile with a receptionist.

My doctor liked vacations, he told me so when I first met him, explaining how he liked to travel to Hawaii with his family, now that his kids were a little older. He was also fond of Italy. I knew those things about him, but he knew almost nothing about me. He was decades into his career and had the detached arrogance of someone who has seen it all. He seemed to view me as an archetype—"The Young Patient"—and treated me according to script. When I did see him, he routinely reminded me how lucky I was to be trying to conceive so young. It was true, I knew, but I didn't like being dismissed because of it. I had 32-year-old eggs and no obvious reproductive challenges, so IVF should just work, right? Only it didn't. One time. Two times. Three times. Fail, fail, fail.

The lack of answers was also taking a toll on Tim, who is a fixer through and through. At the time he was working as a consultant, someone hired by companies, industries, even governments to assess bottom lines and structuring and policies in the interest of helping them function more strategically and profitably. Solving problems was his actual job. Tim is not anxious, he is not a worrier, he does not get ambiguous "bad feelings" or lose sleep over hypotheticals. He is not guided by irrational superstitions—a need to put on one's left shoe before her right, or habitually trace the same set of words in the same well-worn order, or tick off each individual tong on a mascara wand before floating it up through lashes. I have a million of these microscopic, private compulsions, nonsensical little rules to which I have ascribed undue power. My psyche unwittingly invents them with a belief that *if* I repeat each of these behaviors, *then* I will keep Bad Things from happening; the world will continue to spin on its axis. These oddities have both kept me safe and held me hostage since I was a little girl.

Which is all to say that while Tim and I share values and humor and an uncanny ability to choose the same entrée off a restaurant menu, the neural sparks tearing through each of our brains are careening down entirely different tracks.

"Hey," I said, glancing up as my husband appeared through the doorway.

"Hey." He kissed the top of my head. "What's up?"

I shook my head. "Nothing. How was your day?"

His reply, somewhere between a mumble and a mutter, was indecipherable.

"Whad'you say?"

More quiet, indistinct sounds, as if they were only intended for him to hear.

"What?" I said it louder, so deeply annoyed. He did this all the time, spoke under his breath, emitting noise from his throat instead of words from his lips, often in the direction opposite my face, so that I couldn't make out any of it.

"It was fine." That he said loud and clear, annoyed right back. Then his delivery softened. "Just busy, this whole week has been really bad, I didn't eat lunch until four o'clock."

"We have those bars you could bring, just so you have something…" I trailed off as Tim nodded, before moving on to my perennial Topic A. "Ugh, this doctor…"

"What?" Tim asked with a tinge of fear, bracing for whatever fresh outrage I had to share.

"I mean nothing new happened, I just deeply hate him. He's so useless."

"Yeah, I mean he's awful," Tim said, the doctor's terribleness a fact so incontestable as to make him lose interest in the conversation. *Why are we talking about this again?*

I pursed my lips and slanted my eyes. "But like, *no*," I pushed back, indignant. "I cannot just accept that. He's just not going to care? He's not going to look deeper to try to find the underlying issue, because what should be working isn't and he—"

Tim cut me off, impatient. "But you're not going to get—"

"Excuse me," my voice came out strong and forceful, overtaking his. "Can I finish my thought?" He went quiet. "I was speaking. I understand you think what you have to say is more important but it's incredibly rude." There was silence as the room expanded, both of us collecting ourselves. I took a breath, looking down at the table. "My point is that I think we've arrived at a place where the odds don't actually matter. I get that numerically it's bound to happen but how many times is it going to take for both of you to see that our experience is putting us outside of the expected trajectory here? You want to solve it, you want the numbers to make sense, but they literally don't."

When I looked up Tim held my eyes, taking an exaggerated beat to ensure I was finished speaking. "So, what exactly would you like me to do?" he finally said, each word its own icy challenge. "Should we just keep fucking talking about it? Is that helping? What is it that I'm supposed to say?" His was a pedestal of rationality; in these moments, the arrogance with which he stared down at me seemed to set the whole world on fire.

"I don't know!" I was wild now. "I want to have a conversation! And I'm supposed to be trying to relax and this isn't fucking helping!"

The uncertainty, reliably maddening, tonight, had us both plain *mad*. I wanted the comfort and commiseration of poring over this topic, both of us positing theories as to what, why, how all of this was happening, to be listened to, to feel *in it* together. For Tim, talking was pointless. He wanted to fucking fix it.

After our third unsuccessful round, Tim and I finally brought all our frustrations to a formal sit-down with our doctor. My husband, buffed and pressed for the office afterward, leaned back, one oiled Oxford atop the opposite knee, perpetually self-possessed and determined to get answers. I sat toward the front of my seat, two feet flat on the floor, thumb and pointer finger pressing against the meat of my other palm. Let's start by recapping everything that's happened so far, the doctor said, as we nodded and listened with increasing annoyance while he attached his eyes to the computer screen, his hand assuredly maneuvering the mouse as he scrolled through my chart, feigning familiarity with the most raw and painful details of our lives.

As I faced him, asking my questions, expressing my confusion and pain, the doctor did not see me—he never had—and while he talked and talked, saying nothing, my instinct was not to scream, or to flail, or to shake his shoulders until his eyes finally took me in; it was to make myself even more unseeable. I didn't stop until I was a pile of clothes in the chair opposite his.

When he misquoted how many embryos we had remaining, I corrected him, my voice coming out forceful and urgent, giving me a jolt when I heard it. "It's three, actually," I said, my skin burning with insult. "We have three embryos left." Unmoved, he continued, this disinterested stranger offering me a refresher course in my own life. When it came time to discuss the future, he broke the news that the embryology lab would be closing for a few weeks, and because we were planning to genetically test our next round of embryos, our earliest possible transfer would be more than two months away. It was incomprehensible, to wait that long. "This is everything to us,"

I choked out toward the end of that appointment. I was begging him to care.

We left in a hurry, the urgent need to cry somewhere away from this doctor pulling me toward the elevator. By the time Tim and I spilled onto the street and into the late October sunshine, my tears were unrecognizably wild, coming from someplace inside me I hadn't known existed. Standing on the sidewalk, arms limply wrapped around each other, Tim tried to reassure me. "We'll figure it out."

I felt certain of nothing but this: We had to do better.

Our health insurance was through Tim's job and covered a staggering percentage of treatment costs; they were willing to pay for all the rounds we could stomach. I was profoundly aware that even among women who are lucky enough to be covered for some assisted reproductive technology, the benefits available to us were very much outside the norm. Our first doctor didn't know that, though—he knew so little about us—and he oversaw those three embryo transfers with such little thought or regard for what the financial, physical, and emotional costs might be. The coverage we had done nothing to deserve; greater care, I believed, every woman was entitled to.

Back at home I grabbed my computer and stabbed at the keys, typing in the name of another Manhattan clinic I had heard good things about. I read through doctor bios, called offices to inquire about waitlists, and scoured online reviews. There was one young doctor a few months into his practice who seemed familiar somehow. He didn't have decades of experience but he had impressive degrees, a kind face and a mission statement I loved, about providing empathy in addition to exceptional medical care. His goal, he said, was to customize treatment for each patient. When I called, his receptionist told me we could see him in less than three weeks. I took the appointment.

That weekend Tim and I stood along a sun-dappled, brownstone-lined street in Brooklyn and watched the New York City Marathon. We were awed by the elite runners, their ease and fluidity; the athletes with disabilities racing on handcycles, whose arms churned relentlessly to propel them forward; the blind competitors, whose eyes could not see the course before them, but whose ears registered every distinct cheer from the crowd, feeling their way, step by step, all 26.2 miles. It was something to behold, by all appearances ordinary people, young and old, all asking their muscles and hearts to join them in their quest to achieve a superlative physical feat, the glory of the human spirit right there on that street, the human body rising up to meet it.

On this stretch of the marathon route, along Lafayette Avenue just past mile 8, you will find a group of men playing the bongo drums. Tim and I like to stand across the road from them, because the steady power of beating hands—rhythmic, synchronous—creates a vibration in the air, in the body. Nestled inside the kinetic crowd, among spectators balancing children on shoulders, hands clutching steaming cups of coffee, hoisting signs above their heads, Tim and I craned our necks, scanning the road for my friend, Sheila and Tim's friend, Tony. We cheered loudly as they passed, jumping excitedly as our eyes settled on them in the mass of runners, then went back to yelling for hundreds of strangers. In a city whose hum of life is so steady, there is something astonishing about the pulse of this particular day. The heart soars. The soul is stirred. Everything seems possible.

Eventually, we headed home, a tingle across my palms from all the clapping, the echo of bongos in my ears.

That night, darkness descended with a thud. We had turned back the clocks the evening before, and the disappearance of daylight was sudden, profound. It left a void; a sense of something having been stolen right out from under us. Tim, who had gone to a post-race party, walked in quietly, said hello and retreated to the couch, soundlessly pulling up football on TV. "What?" I asked. He looked up at me and the answer came out dully. "Justin's having twins."

We were 33 and had seen many friends get pregnant. But this time, I could read on Tim's face, was different for him. I had miscarried earlier that weekend. We had just found out our third round of IVF had failed. We felt hopeless in the hands of our doctor. And Justin, a friend of Tim's from college, and his wife Kate, were having twins. *Two* babies. As we sat in silence, Tim's eyes turned glassy, blotchy patches spread from his temples.

While we'd mutually lamented the pregnancy news of friends in the past, the sting of it had always belonged to me. This—raw emotion, pain, and grief belonging to Tim—was new. "I haven't really told any of those guys what's been going on with us, but I know they have an idea," he said. "I know they were all looking at me when Justin told us, and it all just makes me feel so alone. I want to be ok, but I'm not." He looked right at me. "I'm not ok."

I was sitting beside him on the couch now. "I'm really sorry," I said. "It's all so isolating, it really is. And I—I don't know, I feel like we're just watching everyone move forward in their lives while we are so stuck." Tim was staring straight ahead, the depth of his sadness occupying space in the room. It was quiet for a while, Sunday night football flashing on mute. Then, in the way two humans are a living ecosystem, a never-ending push/pull between them, reacting and responding to each other at every turn, I instinctively compensated for Tim's despondency. "I really think this new doctor is the answer for us. I think it's going to change everything."

I had first suggested the idea of switching clinics a few days earlier, after that last meeting with our doctor. At the time Tim had been supportive of me looking into it, but I could tell he wasn't convinced. Now, he expressed his hopelessness in full. "Honestly," he started, the dejection in his voice pale, listless. "Why would a new doctor be any different? I legitimately don't believe anyone will be able to help us and I'm really tired of getting my hopes up and being disappointed. I have no interest in going to a new doctor. It's a waste of time. I don't want to do it."

On a different day, it would have been an argument, a fundamental disagreement about this very high-stakes next step in our process. But he was too sad, and I was too taken aback at his sadness, to argue. So we hugged, and we left it alone. "You don't have to come with me to the appointment if you don't want to," I offered. "But I'm going to go and meet him. We owe it to ourselves to attempt this process with a doctor who could actually take a close look at our situation and come up with a real plan. And if we don't like him then we'll go from there."

Two weeks later, with some air between us and the darkness of that evening at home, Tim and I were both sitting across from this new doctor, nervous and expectant and waiting for—what? Answers? Hope? Something. "I am so sorry for everything you have been through," he began, grave and earnest, looking straight into my eyes. "I know it's been a lot." I didn't know what exactly I was hoping to hear or how badly I needed to hear it, but with those first words out of his mouth all the tension that had been building inside me, the pressure I felt to be vigilant about my own care, the compulsion to research my own theories and treatments, the pain of being invisible to my previous doctor as he walked by me in the hallway and didn't recognize me as his patient, the burning need to be *seen*, not as a 30-something who was a promising candidate for IVF but as a woman who was suffering—in that moment, I settled back in my chair and reflexively let all of it go.

He asked me to recap everything that had happened thus far. He knew the details from my medical records, but he wanted to hear my experience of living it. My voice mattered to him. When I got to the part about my ovaries being PCOS-ish, he stopped me.

"You don't have PCOS," he said assuredly, punctuating his point by adding, "Do you have weight gain, hair growth, any of that?" I shook my head. "You don't have PCOS." In an instant, he struck down the only kinda-sorta diagnosis I had ever kinda-sorta been given. One that, in my need to understand what was happening, I had clung to—reading books on the topic, altering my diet and lifestyle accordingly, plunging deep into the rabbit hole, grasping, desperately, for control. This man was everything we were looking for in a doctor, and he was going to take good care of us; I knew it wholeheartedly, and I could tell Tim did too. But still—he had no answers. He was the one, after all, who filled out my Assessment that day. Who left all 80 boxes unchecked.

I had long ago cast myself as the heroine in a PCOS story, jumping into a narrative that seemed to have a clear structure, a definitive arc. Now I no longer knew what kind of story I was in. Was it a tale of perseverance, of a couple determined beyond reason to keep fighting, who would ultimately be rewarded with the baby they were so desperate for? Or was this a drama of madness, two people banging their heads against the wall, repeating the same painful process again and again until they simply could endure no more? It could go either way. We would not know until the final chapter was written. The outcome alone would make the distinction.

# Ambition

"Hi Amy, it's Kim Kardashian."

*Gasp.*

Pause. Rewind. Play.

"Hi Amy, it's Kim Kardashian."

Without knowing what words were coming next, this was already far and away the most memorable voicemail I'd ever received. Kim had called from her own (unblocked) number, not patched in through a PR rep, just dialed me from her cellphone, the very one I'd seen her thumbs punching on nearly every episode of *Keeping Up with the Kardashians.* Our interview was supposed to have taken place the previous day, but lines had gotten crossed and her rep hadn't been able to reach her. Now, without warning, there she was, recorded on my voicemail, offering an apology for the issue yesterday, and sharing her personal number for me to call back. I stood up in my cubicle and asked for everyone within earshot to please come listen.

It was six years prior to the mess of infertility and despite how regularly my job as an entertainment editor for the magazine required me to do these celebrity phone interviews—"phoners" as I learned to call them—they never stopped making me sweat. I'd test and re-test my recorder, compulsively confirming that the battery was full and the memory wasn't. And then I'd sit and wait, engaging in the mental equivalent of pacing as I reviewed my list of questions and played out mock responses in my head. The window of time allotted was usually tight—10 minutes, maybe 15—and I was acutely aware that I had one chance to get it right, ask every possible question, pull out revealing tidbits no one had ever heard, give the star space to share and make her feel at ease enough to open up. But Kim—surely we were tight enough that I could now call her that—was eager to talk and seemed in no rush. When we hung up, I could feel the sweaty heat from my cheek clinging to the receiver, my face always insistent on betraying my nerves. But I'd delivered, and though more deadlines loomed, I gave myself a beat to return to earth.

My first job—shelving books at my small-town public library—was a far cry from the glamour of meeting and interviewing celebrities from my cubicle in Times Square. Technically, it wasn't a real job because I was 12 years old and therefore not yet legally eligible to work. But I was that kind of kid, hesitant to jaywalk but eager for responsibility, so I offered my shelving services for free. I'd pedal over on my cobalt blue 10-speed, haul the front tire into the rack out front, then make my way inside to find my assignment for the day, a metal cart full of returned books, each one needing to be slid into place. I preferred working in YA, naturally, on account of home shelf advantage; I'd practically memorized those aisles and could distribute the contents of an entire cart in no time. Opposite the checkout desk was the adult section, where I dreaded the dense nonfiction titles, their thick, musty spines making the Dewey Decimal System seem especially daunting.

My favorite spot was the soundless, far back aisle of the children's section, opposite row after row of yellow spines with blue lettering: Nancy Drew. I had read every installment but still found pleasure in their company, in the sight of the old-fashioned cover art featuring the girl detective in a skirt suit and 1930s hair flip, flashlight in hand, each hardcover well-worn, edges frayed as if the copies themselves were clues, things unearthed. Nancy brought intrigue to my life and taught me the kind of person I'd like to be:

someone with ingenuity and good sense, someone who was independent and unafraid. It was in her company that the concept of a mystery first toyed with my mind. Every one of her cases ebbed and flowed through a familiar rhythm, leading to the exhale of the final page, a satisfying conclusion reached, wherein everything finally made sense.

When I wasn't shelving or squirreled away in the stacks with Nancy, I could be found listening to younger kids give verbal book reports for the summer reading program. For this part of my gig, I got to sit behind the very official-looking desk in the children's section, and a boy or girl, maybe seven or eight, would pull up a miniature chair and describe things such as plot and characters, their favorite part or if they would recommend it to a friend. I can't remember if I asked a standard set of questions, or if it was more off-the-cuff than that, but I know I paid close attention to those reports and relished the authority of bestowing a sticker for each book successfully read. I liked the feeling of things behind that desk. Asking questions, listening to answers, being surrounded by words. I liked the tidiness of an empty cart, the order of stocked shelves, the satisfaction of knowing I'd been the one to return the books where they belonged. I liked how it felt being out on my own— even if it was only at the library a couple of quiet blocks away from the street where I lived.

***

That first year at the magazine, when I was 24 years old, my nervous system jangled every time the phone rang, my stomach clenching when I'd glance down to see a 310 or 323 number, meaning Los Angeles. It was almost always a celebrity PR rep calling to discuss an actress or musician we might want to feature, or negotiate the details of an upcoming photo shoot or interview. I was fielding the calls for the magazine's entertainment director, one of my two bosses, and I was always aware that these were *important people*, many of them brusque and terrifying. I worked hard to be unflappable in these exchanges, wouldn't want them to catch wind that deep down I was someone whose temperament was better suited to receiving overdue books at the library, so as I greeted and patched them through to my boss, I aimed to mimic their directness while maintaining some warmth. But even their assistants, some of whom I'd speak with regularly, seemed as though they could eat me for breakfast.

There were certain calls from within the magazine that inspired fear as well; powerful, sometimes mercurial editors were churning out 12 issues a year, working and re-working stories on impossible deadlines, and they could be intense and intimidating because of the pressure. The level to which it all affected me became apparent one night in 7C, when my roommates and I decided to start watching the show *24*. The ringtone featured throughout each episode had a near-identical cadence and frequency to that of the phone at my desk, and when I heard it, I could feel my whole body seize, cortisol tearing through me, an automatic response inspired by the terror of whoever's curt voice might be on the other end of the line. *Oh my God you guys, I don't think I can watch this!*

Yet I couldn't imagine loving a job more. There hadn't been a "right" college for me, I had yet to meet the "right" person. Not since I'd modeled myself into the second coming of Nancy Drew had I been as sure of anything as I was of this exact job at this exact magazine. As a loyal subscriber and devoted reader, I'd long ago memorized the name of every editor on the masthead. I was already obsessed with movies and television and celebrity culture, so this presented my ideal foray into entertainment journalism. Plus, I'd get to write about fashion—the glamorous cherry on top.

The job didn't happen by accident. I'd set my sights on the role, circling it for years. I fought my way into the industry, applying for (and failing to get) dozens of different entry-level positions until I eventually landed my first gig in the beauty department of a teen magazine before moving on to my dream role. When I got it, the achievement registered as both an inevitability and an impossible dream come true. That girl back at the library would've been so damn proud.

***

By the time I flicked off the cubicle light it had been more than 12 hours since I'd turned it on. The remnants of three deskside meals and a long-ago emptied coffee cup were stuffed in my trash can and I was finally ready to head home, though my day was not nearly over. All those ringing phones, the hours I spent at the photocopy machine compiling binders of celebrity features, meant the actual writing I got to do was crammed in after hours. My fashion copy was due tomorrow, so I'd have to come up with pithy captions to describe several pages worth of dresses and sweaters and jewelry before I could go to sleep. Hours and hours invested in giving the world cleverness in the vein of *Pearls gone wild!* to accompany an edgy necklace with several tangled strands of gems and stones (it's harder than it looks, folks!)

"Bye, guys," I called out, to whichever of my friends were still poised over their keyboards. "Bye!" I heard back. "See you tomorrow."

Downstairs, the lobby was empty, museum-like. Throughout the day it was a blur of bodies, photo editors with stacks of images, fashion assistants pushing racks of clothes, everyone in such a hurry. But late in the evening all that remained was the imposing architecture, highlighted by stillness and shadows. Each individual click of my heels echoed through the elevator bank, before I pushed my way through the revolving glass doors and emerged into Times Square, which was neon and throbbing always. I descended the stairs into the subway, hopped the two trains home, and kicked off my boots on the floor of 7C. The TV was on, so I sat down with Tara and Jessie for a bit, then changed into sweats to start in on my last task of the day.

My work tote was a perpetual jumble of crumpled Starbucks receipts, tubes of lip gloss, magazines, and papers, so when, at first glance, my layout wasn't among the clutter, I didn't immediately panic. *Where is it?* I wondered, rifling through everything again, then thought back, certain I had pulled up the file on my desktop and pressed print. I could see it in my mind, a crisp stack atop the printer. But had I actually grabbed it? I must have. Right? My stomach twisted with a dawning realization. Oh my God. I never got it. It was still sitting there. I looked down at my phone. 11p.m. *Fuck fuck fuck.*

Tara came out of the bathroom, face scrubbed and moisturized. "What are you doing?" I was sliding my arms back into my coat. "I left my work on the printer and the pages are due tomorrow," it came out in a flustered, disbelieving choke of emotion and exhaustion. So many tiny captions to write, about peasant blouses and strappy sandals, so much small and satisfying wordplay to come up with that perhaps an entire handful of people would read. "I have to go back and get them, turn around, come back home, and *then* start writing." "Jesus," Tara looked horrified. "That really sucks." I watched as she made her way into her room to fall asleep to an episode of *Friends*, then hurried downstairs to hail a cab. My disposable income did not allow for traveling this way, but at this hour, under these circumstances, being able to get to Times Square and back relatively quickly was the only thing keeping me from completely losing it.

Though I'd spent plenty of evenings and weekends at the office, never had I seen it so desolate. The censored lights flicked on as I stalked toward the printer and grabbed my papers, cold and unassuming in their orderly little pile, as though they had not just completely fucked me over. My fury softened once they were in my possession, more still once I was in the back of a cab heading home, this enraging errand nearly complete. I resisted the urge to get a jump on the writing by crafting captions in my head (*Strap happy?*

*Strappy-go-lucky?*), instead leaning toward the window to take in the midnight lights, aglow up and down every avenue, along infinite blocks, the glittering energy of this city discernible, infectious, inspiring. Back at home, for real this time, I climbed into bed, propped myself up against some pillows, and got to work.

\*\*\*

Though the magazine world came with an endless stream of perks—flying to Miami to interview Gabrielle Union, never mind the parties and screenings, filming an appearance on a soap opera, and the goodies of every possible persuasion that found their way to the wondrous free-for-all known as the "giveaway table"—nothing compared to seeing words I'd written in print. Sentences born from my brain, there on glossy paper, knowing they'd made it past multiple rounds of edits and met the exacting standards of the powers that be. Once I proved I could handle captions, I was given opportunities to write longer features—fitness, beauty, and fashion stories, and celebrity pieces galore. With grit and will and hard work, I felt certain, absolutely anything was possible.

\*\*\*

Six years later, I was channeling all of the early ambition that had kept me up all night writing copy into a new pursuit: becoming pregnant. The markers were different—follicle size, embryo grades, hCG count—but I was hungry for success all the same, and as I went under, my ovaries brimming with eggs, ready for retrieval, I guessed at what today's tally might be. Within seconds I was hovering beyond myself, trapped within a cloud of artificial sleep. The anesthesia for my egg retrievals was light and brief, and it couldn't have been more than 15 minutes before my ovaries had been emptied, my eyelids were fluttering open, and my hands were accepting apple juice and graham crackers.

"How do you feel, honey?" A nurse asked, handing me the snack.

"I'm good." I was groggy, but as long as I was waking up from the anesthesia, then it was true; I was good.

There were crumbs gathered in the creases of my hospital gown when she came back to check my vitals. "Quite a resting heart rate on you," she said, giving me an affectionate pat. "My dear, that is *low*." My resting heart rate was a number I'd given approximately zero thought to, but based on the nurse's reaction I could tell it should be a significant source of pride. "Are you a runner?" she asked, before answering her own question. "You must be a runner."

It had been ages since I'd been called out for anything in me that was exceptional.

"Yes," I was blushing, warmed by her words. "I am."

I was starving, in those days, for accomplishment. Though at that point I was still working, at the wellness website, infertility had stolen my willingness to care about it. Any potential for success hinged on my body, where I'd experienced no wins at all. I had thrown my whole self into the process of trying to get pregnant and been rewarded with unending failure. This absurd, unforeseen achievement, the news of my low resting heart rate, puffed me up for days. (Caption: *Best of the rest? Rest in show?*)

The other triumphant figure I received that day was 19, as in the number of mature eggs I'd produced (Coverline: *19 ways your body loves you back!*). There were plenty to freeze, so I didn't need to stimulate again for several months, not, it turned out, until I failed enough to want to switch doctors. At the new clinic, the routine was the same, only the recovery involved cranberry juice instead of apple, curtained-off stalls instead of an open room full of gurneys. The stalls reminded me of the cubicles in which my friends and I had worked at the magazine, where our voices would float over the top of the partitions, where we could hear each other chew salad and book travel plans. Today, the women on either side of me had names and faces I would never know. At some point, my doctor's voice became audible alongside the patient to my right. He was speaking quietly but still I could hear him, and I could tell the news wasn't good. "So, I'm disappointed with how it went today. We were only able to get three eggs." I couldn't make out her response, but I didn't need to.

The slide of metal against metal as the doctor drew back my curtain a while later, angling himself through the gap. He asked how I was doing before offering up my results. "We retrieved 24 eggs," he announced proudly. "Now they won't all be mature, we'll have a final number later, but it went very, very well." The part of me that's competitive—with myself, with others—beamed, my mouth dangling open with the knowledge that I had been an undeniable success. I internalized this news as though the number wasn't luck, or good fortune, or happenstance, but a reflection of something deserving in me. I'd worked hard, and I'd *produced*. Still, I hoped the woman who'd gotten three eggs had already clocked out of her cubicle, or at the very least couldn't hear what had gone down in mine.

\*\*\*

At the magazine, I'd accepted every assignment I was offered, any chance for another clip, a new experience that might challenge me, the more daunting, the better. When I eventually quit working, to immerse myself fully in my new role as Fertility Patient, I discovered a surprising range of my old professional skills applied: conducting research, organizing and synthesizing information, posing questions. I was allegedly working as a freelance writer, but unlike at the magazine, I said no to everything. No to one-off writing assignments and extended in-office gigs. No to former colleagues and complete strangers. My editor friends seemed confused: *Are you sure? We can be flexible on the deadline? Ok, well let me know if you change your mind.* I grappled with how wrong it felt to turn down work, so besides posing questions to doctors, I also posed some to myself. Being a magazine writer/editor was the only career I'd ever seriously considered; if I no longer wanted that, if I no longer felt curiosity and passion for it, then I didn't have a clue what might be next. In my notebook, I scribbled some questions:

*What do I need from a job?*

*What do I want from it?*

*Drive? —> is that numb b/c I'm numb*

The truth is, I didn't want to write, or interview celebrities, or come up with clever captions about fashion. Now, I had a new ambition. And to that end, I was as driven as ever. The single-mindedness that had characterized my days at the magazine, grinding as hard as I could, the first one through the door in the morning, staying past dinner to churn out the best stuff I was capable of, it was still there, simply redirected toward getting pregnant. If ambition is an amalgamation of focus and sacrifice, taking risks and refusing to give up, then I qualified, no doubt. It's just seen in a different light when done in the pursuit of motherhood than in the name of professional excellence. Now there was one singular force driving my every decision—caption: *Mom genes.*

\*\*\*

Gwyneth Paltrow wasn't among the celebrities I had the chance to interview, but she would have been my ultimate. She'd been an object of fascination for me since I was in high school, when I admired her cool style and cooler attitude enough to wear the knockoff of her pink Oscars dress to my senior prom. So, when I heard advance tickets were available for her cookbook-signing event at a Williams Sonoma store in the city, a few friends and I collectively squealed, then were lucky enough to score a few. I was still working as an editor at the website at the time, and when the big day finally came, I ran out of work calling, "Bye guys, gotta go see Gwyneth!"

"Tell her we said hi!" someone hollered back.

My friends and I rushed out of our respective offices and converged outside the store, stepping in line with our pre-ordered copies of *It's All Good* pressed against our chests. Inside, waiting to greet us one-by-one, sat Gwyneth, as polished as the cover of her book, hair smooth and bright, skin buffed to a sheen, blue oxford forming two daggers beside her collar bone. When it was my turn, one of my friends snapped a picture of me handing her my book. I had imagined mentioning how much I loved her recipe for Tortilla Española, how it tasted so much like my grandmother's, but in the end, I think I said something more articulate, something along the lines of, "hi." And, "thank you," as she smiled back warmly, scrawling her name and an oversized heart on the book's title page. Though our encounters were all of 10 seconds, they became far longer stories as my friends and I spilled back onto the street, giddily bumping up against each other, talking over each other, before heading to dinner on an A-list high. We were romanced by the buds of early April, the pink dusky light, the scent of spring in the city.

\*\*\*

By the time I finally pulled my signed cookbook off the shelf, it was dotted with dust, the spine snapping open as though startled by my touch. I was overhauling my diet in hopes of getting pregnant, and Gwyneth's recipes jumped to mind. Her philosophy was that wholesome food could be as flavorful and delicious as it is nourishing.

Perhaps because of all the ways it stood in contrast to the cold, clinical nature of IVF, or perhaps because I couldn't imagine that Gwyneth herself had ever failed at anything, the book pulled me in. I read recipes for roasted vegetables with the attentiveness I'd give literary prose, I lingered on images of vibrant produce shot in natural, golden light, of Gwyneth looking serene and earthy, all of it inviting me into the healthy, happy life I was seeking. Cooking my way through the pages became a kind of project: dicing, whisking, searing, simmering. Vegan risotto swimming with peas and greens, bright beet salad, turkey chili studded with sweet potatoes, each offering more than a meal, more even than the nourishment I hoped would act as medicine. The cooking was a goal unto itself, a way to occupy myself on long, empty afternoons when everyone else was at work. Besides, are you ever really alone if you have Gwyneth?

It was strange, recalling the life I'd been living when I'd first gotten the book I now held in my hands. The afternoon I'd dashed out of work, hastily fired off emails on the subway uptown, embraced friends, walked and laughed for blocks afterward as we headed to dinner at the latest hip place. I had been ambitious in my career back then, but also for experiences—I said *yes*. Now all of that had fallen away in service of what had proven to be a quieter, lonelier ambition, an ambition powerful enough to have overtaken all the others. Oddly, the pages of Gwyneth Paltrow's cookbook were the one and only place where my former and present ambitions could stand in their conflicting, competing truths alongside each other. Gwyneth, actress, wellness-mogul, vagina-candle-impresario, was maybe the only one to understand all past and present versions of me.

Often while cooking, I was standing by for the phone to ring. I seemed to be perpetually awaiting a call: from my doctor with an update, or a nurse with the evening's medication instructions. Swirling leeks through broth, hip pressed up against the stove, the sole of one bare foot resting alongside the ankle of another, I'd have an eye on the phone, my spiral notebook close by. Sometimes the calls with the nurses were straightforward, I'd find out what story that day's blood work told and how much medication to draw into a syringe later. Other times I'd have questions to ask, words scribbled in my notebook, so much like my interview prep from way back when. *Based on my blood, do you have a guess as to when my transfer will be? My insurance is mailing my injectables, but the pills and patches fall under my prescription card; would you mind calling those into my pharmacy instead?* The nurses made how many versions of those calls to how many women every afternoon; if I didn't pick up, it was next to impossible to dial back and actually get someone.

For this reason, I got into the habit of taking my phone with me into the shower. Not the actual stall, but into the bathroom, placing it beside the sink where I could keep my eyes on it. I'd draw back the curtain every 15 seconds or so, eventually succumbing to an impulse to leave it pulled open entirely. Heat escaped, water sprayed, but it allowed the face of my phone to be visible even while I sudsed up my hair and rinsed off my body and risked damaging the device itself with all those droplets.

It was all in the name of being available for that precious handful of seconds. More than once, though, the call—inexplicably? inevitably?—managed to come through without my noticing. All that vigilance and I wound up with a voicemail anyway, eliciting the same sort of panic and angst a missed call from a celebrity publicist used to all those years ago.

"Hi Amy, it's Nurse Jen."

*Gasp.*

"I have your medication instructions for tonight."

Heat clung to my face as I listened, not from the steam of the shower or the soup simmering in the kitchen, but from the agony of the untouched notebook nearby. The one whose questions would go unanswered again.

# Shame

***

Six eyeballs appeared unannounced, suspended high in the air on the other side of my living room window. I wasn't prepared to see faces up against the glass, living on the seventh floor and all, but today there were three of them. I had been caught.

I wasn't doing much of anything, technically, though that was the point. It had been only a couple of weeks since I'd quit my job, so this September weekday found me at home, un-showered, in workout clothes, all by myself, the channel still set to the network of the morning news. I hadn't thought much about the TV being on, or what I was or wasn't doing, until the dangling ropes adjusted and the three men repairing the façade of our building hiccupped into place behind the couch. Their presence, being *seen*, snapped me to. I lunged for the remote. Had they noticed the screen flickering? There could be a baby napping in another room, my mind pointed out, racing to justify this scene. Or, I reasoned, if I happened to work nights, I would have every right to be home alone right now.

Anything other than the truth: that I was a privileged white woman in her top floor loft apartment, not working, not caring for a child, not contributing in any way, just taking up space, merely existing between costly infertility treatments, nearly all of which were covered by a first-class insurance policy through her husband's elite consulting job. Tens—possibly hundreds—of thousands of dollars worth of procedures, medications, even chunks of my acupuncture and therapy bills, all taken care of. I not only had no job but a golden ticket.

In those early days at home, my new "lifestyle" still taking shape, the shame overwhelmed me unexpectedly and often. It wasn't that I regretted my decision to stop working, I just didn't recognize or particularly like the person who'd made it. This useless, solitary soul, apparently devoid of ambition to further her stalled career, lacking work ethic and intellectual curiosity, content to live off her husband's salary, loafing her way through a world full of decent, productive people. I'd pass them as they ran out on a lunch break or rustled up snacks for babies in strollers, and felt sure they were all really *seeing* me, that my worthlessness could be observed, a radioactive silhouette in the crowd.

I also devoted significant energy to imagining the perspectives of my former bosses and colleagues, the brilliant, accomplished editors who had taught me so much about journalism and storytelling, about drive and ambition, who had seen potential in me and invested in me, offered support and mentorship. What did they make of me now? *I guess she's not who we thought she was,* I imagined them musing. *Clearly she's not a hard worker, someone with promise, someone who's going places. Her priorities are...different.* And now there were six eyes out the window, witnessing the dead air of my day up close. It didn't just look bad; it felt bad.

As my unexpected company dangled, I pretended not to see them, averting my gaze, grabbing the computer to feign busyness, retreating to the kitchen to slather an apple in almond butter. Anything to deny the hollow idleness they had interrupted. To return to it would be an admission that I was exactly who I appeared to be.

*** 

*Shame.* The word escaped my mouth heavily, more accident than decision. But once it was out there, I leaned into it. "I feel so much shame." My therapist and I were still getting to know each other, I began seeing her when I switched to the new doctor, and that confession, those words hanging in her office between us, was our first real moment. She replied slowly, her thoughts unspooling. "It's interesting to me to hear you say that, because shame is an emotion that seems to take into account an outside perspective. It is only felt in front of others. To experience it, you need an audience." I nodded through tears, agreeing with her assessment objectively, while also not knowing what to make of it. My shame was so private, so deeply entombed, so wholly and completely mine, that I could not for the life of me conceive of who, exactly, was my audience. Whose gaze was burning me up?

\*\*\*

For a long time my grandmother—and my parents for that matter—knew nothing of my struggles to have a baby. They never asked, and I never shared. Instead we all gathered for Christmas, hugging and kissing and toasting our way around the unspoken understanding that Tim and I hoped to have kids one day. But soon enough the logical sense of when it would happen had passed. And then more time passed still. It was apparent something was going on, but we were all committed to letting it go unsaid. Whenever we gathered for a holiday I felt the strain of unmet expectations, and the discomfort of the unacknowledged truth. I took my seat among the women in my family, three generations of mothers—my grandmother, my mom, my sister, Stephanie—who had all gotten pregnant without issue, each changed by the experience of growing and birthing and raising a child, a certain spiritual connection between them, of which I knew nothing.

Everything else was the same as it had ever been, or, at least, as similar as it could be since my grandfather had died. The same menu: shrimp cocktail, lasagna, chocolate mousse. The same red checked ribbon encircling the slats of the banister, the same tattered copies of *The Dolls' Christmas* and *'Twas the Night Before Christmas* propped open, as they might be in the children's section of the library, the same nutcrackers tall and rigid on the mantle above the same stockings Santa used to fill. My grandparents would arrive in the early afternoon, he in a collared shirt, pressed pants and festive red socks (his favorite color); she in a long strand of pearls atop a silk blouse, either ivory or black, her short hair bouncy and fresh, gold earrings glinting alongside.

Once my grandfather was gone, all the trimmings remained in place, but the feeling in the house was muted, disjointed. Instead of all piling into the TV room, where our cluster of voices had once mingled with Frank Sinatra's Greatest Hits and one televised sporting event or another, my sister, grandmother, and I would, without discussion, slip into the living room one by one, where we arranged ourselves by the fire. The Christmas hearth was a tradition just like all the others, and the promise of warmth and contemplation and memory had a strong, quiet pull.

Stephanie and I would sit beside each other on the loveseat, upholstered in a smooth pine green, sometimes with her daughter on one of our laps. Grandma had stopped dressing up for holidays, her "occasion" look now a velour jumpsuit the color of eggplant, but the pearls were still there, a relic of her former self, and an entire forearm full of gold bangles, which she never went without. She sat across from us, angled toward the fire in a straight-backed chair made of honey-toned wood, the arms clawed like the feet of a bathtub. She was a bit slouched but regal as ever.

At least there by the fire it was Christmas and not Mother's Day, which, unsurprisingly, was the worst holiday of all, for reasons including but not limited to the toast my father gave, which had been tweaked in recent years to indirectly address me. "Let's raise a glass to the mothers," my dad would say at the start of the meal, lifting his Spanish white. "The mothers who are here, the mothers we have lost, and the mothers who are yet to be." He would say this last part with emphasis, then clink my glass purposefully. I was warmed by the generosity in his words—he was determined to include me so that I wouldn't be alone at the table—but it was the heat of shame that burned me up. My sister, always in the seat beside me, was noticeably uncomfortable, recognizing how it must feel to be inadvertently called out on this holiday that quite painfully had nothing to do with me. I cannot say if all the eyes at the table were trained on me during the kicker of the toast, because I had to stare at the tablecloth to survive it.

Mercifully, today, on this Christmas, we would raise our glasses and wish each other a Merry Merry and give a special nod to the people we loved who were gone. Those "in the balcony" as my grandfather would have said, had he not recently become one of them. I could smell the lasagna in the oven as the fire snapped, the rapture of orange flickering across each of our faces. And then my grandmother said it, her voice cutting through the silence. "You know," she began, looking at me pointedly, before turning her eyes back toward the flames, "we're due for a boy around here."

***

The frosted glass door of the clinic swung open every 60 seconds or so and it was difficult to find a seat that would allow for distance between myself and everyone else, ideally facing away from the action. If my seat left me open to the entrance, it was harder to curb the impulse to look up every time a new patient arrived. I'd have to force myself to stare intently at the same outdated *People* magazine, held up high, shielding my face and (fingers crossed!) rendering me invisible, so as to avoid meeting someone's gaze. Or, God forbid, coming face to face with a person I knew.

Despite my attempts to be imperceptible to the naked eye, I'm pretty sure I was, in fact, visible, and probably looked bored, or deeply engrossed in celebrity news, although the flatness in my expression belied the truth; I was suffocating from the panic of a potential run-in. I felt vulnerable and exposed, aware of the omnipresent threat that had the person crossing the threshold been a former co-worker or a girl I'd known growing up, we would have been forced into the awkwardness of close-quarters avoidance, or of acknowledging each other's presence. And that, of course, came with an admission.

There was something disquieting about the shame I experienced in that waiting room, given that all of us were there for the same, objectively harmless reason; attempting to get pregnant with the help of science. If anyone understood what that process really meant, with its complexities and logistics and emotions and demands and isolation and pain, it was the women right here. These were my people! Had this been a legitimate prison cell and not merely a metaphorical one, we would've had all the makings of an incredible gang: Infertile is the new orange is the new black. But the stigma, the hush assigned to it in the world, seemed determined to follow us all the way into treatment. None of us spoke; we barely even acknowledged each other.

I've wondered why I didn't hold my head higher, let my eyes meet someone else's, instead of shrinking down to nothingness in this roomful of strangers all here for the same reason—that we couldn't get pregnant on our own. Was the shame born from an inability to do something commonplace, something meant to be easy, something so many others did without trying too hard? Or was it shame about the physicality of it, a mortification that it was my female parts, ovaries and uterus and reproductive organs, at the center of it all? Perhaps because infertility hinges on those "private places," it feels like something that can't be spoken of. And the things we can't speak of often get heavy.

And yet. The incessant swinging of that frosted door and the long waits to hear my name were also comforting, overwhelming proof that I was not alone.

That made no difference. I sat shrouded in shame all the same.

Sometimes, I'd go to the main clinic, where four elevators opened directly into the waiting area, women spilling out with every ding. Cycle monitoring began at 6:30 a.m., and I tried to get there as early as I could, but even so, it was impossible to find a nook to myself. But at least in the swarm of the larger clinic, I felt a degree of anonymity, shielded by the crowd.

There, one early weekend morning, my eyes drifted up from my copy of *People* and swept across the long, sun-filled chamber, where they tripped over a face I recognized. *Oh my God.* I swallowed. It had happened. The dull buzz of activity halted, the room blurred, my focus zeroed in. It was a girl from college. An acquaintance—I couldn't guess at her last name—but we'd seen each other at a party in the city a few years back where we'd talked easily for a while. She was nice. And now, life had brought us both to this waiting room. It shouldn't have been stunning—I had anticipated this moment with every swing of that frosted door, every ding of the elevator—but here I was, stunned nevertheless.

My instinct for avoidance, and all those months practicing being invisible, had prepared me. My head snapped back down so I could become deeply absorbed in my reading material (the new cast of *Dancing with the Stars?* Tell me more!), and it stayed there while I used peripheral vision to make sure I had a sense of where she was in the room. A nurse called my name and I hurled myself out of the seat, then stared intently at my phone when it was time to head back toward the elevator bank and exit through the lobby, never lifting my eyes from the screen.

I didn't entertain the idea of trying to meet this woman's eyes or going over to say hello. The discomfort of sharing space in that room, and the effort required to pretend that neither of us was really there, was wholly consuming. Besides, for all I knew she, too, was trying to hide. But afterward, once I was safely out in the world again, my gang affiliation no longer visible to the naked eye, I wondered if she would have welcomed a smiling face, an exchange of numbers, a suggestion to grab coffee. There was no denying that I needed an infertility friend. Maybe she did too.

***

Perhaps if I'd had that friend, someone who shared in this particular pain of mine, I would have been better able to gauge the degree to which infertility had ripped me open. As it was, alone, I struggled to put it into context. This wasn't life or death (or incarceration), I'd remind myself, it was a challenge to shake off. People in every corner of this world were suffering, and I was so fortunate in a million different ways. So why, then, had I allowed this experience to bring me to my knees? Could it be that I was overreacting? Wallowing? Why couldn't I just be more grateful for everything I had? How had I let this tear me apart?

One quiet autumn night the TV was set to *60 Minutes* while Tim and I ate dinner at our kitchen counter, the world chilly and dark beyond our windows. The scene was ordinary, so similar to every other Sunday, but on this night, as I recall it, the show was profiling the Make a Wish Foundation, telling the story of a child dying of cancer, a child the organization had surprised with a trip to Australia—his dream. From the jump, this sweet boy learning the news in the gymnasium of his school, hugging his mom with disbelief and elation, the specific look on his face—innocent and incredulous and full of gratitude—stirred something in me. As the segment progressed and he bounded around down under, exclaiming over the koalas, bursting with joy to be sharing it with his family, the heartrending punch of his story landed blow after blow. It was suffering that crossed into tragedy, punctuated by the wonder of a child. By the time the piece ended and an addendum flashed on the screen to report that the boy had died shortly after his trip, I had long since set down my fork. His was pain so real I couldn't look away.

I suppose I could have allowed myself to mourn for this boy, for the cruelty with which fate had treated him, simply let my heart constrict and expand with grief, all without holding his suffering up next to mine. Instead, pushing tears off my cheeks, I turned with disgust to myself. What problems did I have anyway, my mind spat out. I wasn't dying. Someone I loved wasn't dying. There was food on the table, there was love in my life. What entitled me, with my unending comforts and privilege, to be so devastated simply because I couldn't get pregnant? I was so lost inside of it that I couldn't tell if I had a right to my own heartache.

I have no idea if Tim caught wind of my state of mind as we watched. What I know is that I worked hard to conceal my shame, burying it in the deepest part of me, the hidden center of my being, where it could go about its work corroding my insides. In the echo chamber of my mind, I continued to poke holes in my own sorrow, pushing hard on my bruises to see if they still hurt, to make them hurt. But whenever a nurse called to report another IVF failure, initiating another goodbye to another baby I would never know, I experienced the sort of palpable pain that confirms itself on impact, pain I felt in my heart and in my cells and tissue and flesh and bones. It hurt. So, while it was true that a loved one wasn't dying, it was also true that a hoped-for loved one wasn't living. It wasn't a matter of death, necessarily, but it *was* a matter of life. That had to mean something.

*\*\**

All along, I never stopped revisiting my therapist's question about my shame. Just whose gaze was burning me up? The truth, I believe, is that while no one person was *shaming* me, each set of eyes acted as a pair of floodlights, unwittingly illuminating a dark, depraved cavity where all my most destructive self-beliefs were hidden. The eyes could belong to anyone; anonymous eyes, imagined eyes, or eyes genetically resembling mine, the same grey-blue, with the slight downward slope at the corners. They could be my own eyes in the mirror, or none at all.

The eyes were blameless. Unaware of their power, they never knew that they were casting light on the very worst of me. They never knew they made the shadows dance.

# Grief

**VOLUME I**

One muggy August night a few months after we got engaged, a small group of family and friends gathered in the backyard of Tim's childhood home for our engagement party. There were white lights strung along the border of a tent and card tables arranged cozily, hydrangeas from the garden as centerpieces, our childhood snapshots grinning up from each one. An old rowboat rested on the grass, anchored by the weight of beer and wine and mountains of ice, a display of nautical refrigeration befitting summer in Rhode Island. Curled shrimp were dunked in cocktail sauce, hugs were exchanged warmly, our future toasted and toasted yet again. The party was given by Tim's mom and stepdad, but somehow it was my grandfather who wound up giving a speech that night, and it was he and my grandma who posed for photographs cutting the cake.

That felt exactly right. They were the elder statesman and woman of the party—their 60 years of marriage earning them the kind of relationship clout it takes a lifetime to build, their quiet, palpable love a beacon of what was possible. While we were nervously setting out on this grand adventure of marriage, they, unequivocally, had made it.

It didn't hurt that my grandparents were as vibrant and interesting a couple as you could hope to meet, 80-something or otherwise. My grandma was elegant and sharp-witted, zinging one-liners as she sipped her sauvignon blanc, her slender gold bangles crashing together along her forearm. My grandfather was affable and engaging—a throwback of a man who also had a unique claim on the present. At 87, he still worked five days a week, commuting from the suburbs of New York City to Manhattan where he was a sports cartoonist and columnist for one of the city's newspapers. His close to 70 years on the job had earned him the distinction of being someone who'd created art the day President Kennedy was shot just as he did the day two planes crashed into the World Trade Center. He had covered every major sporting event throughout his tenure (all the mundane ones, too), earned the friendship of iconic athletes from Joe DiMaggio to Muhammad Ali, and been nominated for a Pulitzer.

My grandfather was passionate about his work, he loved life, and he treasured his family. A first generation American whose parents emigrated from Spain and Argentina, he had witnessed struggle and death up close; first, at age 11, when his father died, and then later in the Pacific during WWII, where he fought as a Marine in Saipan and Iwo Jima. And yet his spirit was buoyant. Always quick to laugh, he couldn't help being tickled by this or that, and showing it with his open-mouthed cackle.

It was no wonder, then, that my grandfather forged a special bond with an exuberant kid who'd bounded her way through childhood: me. He loved to tell the story of the ballet recital where I was doing my pliés eagerly enough to pull the barre right over, causing a pile-up of tiny dancers. One Christmas morning I ran up and down the stairs with such vigor, California Raisins nightshirt fluttering behind, alternating between shrieking over the presents under the tree and cajoling my parents out of bed, that eventually I puked all over the floor from the sheer force of my excitement. My grandfather was amused by me; I adored him.

The grandfather/granddaughter love was undeniable, but it was as two writers that our souls truly connected. In the 9th grade I wrote an English paper called "Grandma's Kitchen," describing the warmth and heart of my favorite room in their house. My grandfather, in an expression of his own exuberance, tried to turn my essay into a children's book. "Amy, this is something," he said emphatically in his loving, gravelly way. "I'm not kidding—this ought to *be* something!"

My words were nothing more than a description of how something was always cooking in that kitchen, how the smell would hit you the moment you walked in, how I liked to sit in the wooden chairs with wicker seats as my grandma chopped and stirred. But he proceeded to illustrate them with his drawings, using his pen to memorialize the copper-bottomed pots dangling from the rack overhead and the dish towel that hung just-so in front of the oven. He shopped it to who-knows-how-many publishers, none of whom bit, but that didn't stop him from referring back to it for years ("It should've been a book, Amy; I'm telling you.) One summer during college I spent a day tooling around New York City with my roommate, the highlight of which was a visit to his office, where he introduced me around the newsroom as, "My granddaughter, Amy—the writer!" I laughed, blushing, but with the weight of his voice behind those words, I dared to believe that perhaps someday they could be true.

After graduation, when I was hired for my first magazine job, my entrance into the family business was official; I was a fourth-generation journalist. My great-grandfather had worked for a Spanish newspaper, *La Prensa*, in New York City in the early 1900s, then came my grandfather, followed by my father, who also worked at one of the city's papers, as the sports editor, and now me. I belonged to this very special subset of Gallos, whose careers spanned decades and languages, my work now putting me in the distinguished company of the man I most admired.

Toward the end, when that man got sick, I called to tell him about an article I'd had published in a national magazine, one I'd never previously written for. I was excited and knew he would be too, I thought maybe I could cheer him up. "I wrote about things you should start doing more slowly," I prattled, trying to keep things upbeat, "like chewing, breathing, that kind of thing. It was just a small piece but I'm hoping to start writing for them more." He wheezed a bit, catching his breath, his voice heavier than normal. "That's great, Amy." He followed it up with a simple pronouncement that, from the lips of a dying man, sobered me: "Keep it in the family."

Before all that though, when he was still healthy, my grandfather stood on the patio at Tim's mom's house wearing a teal golf shirt and khakis hiked a little too high, talking off-script in the charming, delightful way only an octogenarian can. He spoke of his long marriage to my grandmother, of how wonderful Tim was, of the comfortable future we would have ("Amy, you're going to live in a big house," he proclaimed, prompting laughter around the yard and mortifying me beyond belief). Eventually, he got around to me. "There's something about Amy," he began. "Her enthusiasm. Her big heart. She's bubbles. And she's the blithe spirit of our family." At these words, this demonstrative love, from the *actual* blithe spirit of our family, I wiped my eyes.

There is a photo of him and me from the party, smiling at each other as we said goodnight, his hand cupping my chin; the last picture we ever took together.

Nine months later he was gone, and a few years after that, the bright, effervescent girl he'd spoken of was gone, too. The magazine editor who would scramble to leave the office in time to meet her grandparents at a restaurant or a cocktail party across town; who would apply lipstick and slip into her highest heels beforehand knowing her chic and exacting grandmother would notice; who would talk animatedly about what stories she was working on, what adventures she was having as a 20-something in the glittering city, who would pepper them with questions about life, leaning across the table intently as they answered, trying to absorb every word.

As the losses piled up—the loss of my work, the loss of my friends, as they started families around me, the loss of my sense of self—the woman my grandfather spoke of was swallowed up, the various losses eclipsing each other, becoming so numerous that there wasn't time to grieve. Instead, the lines between each individual wound began to blur until I felt as if I was walking around with a huge gaping hole that couldn't be filled or fixed but that I simply had to live with.

Now, still living in the most glamorous city in the world, I rarely left our apartment other than to sit in oppressively neutral waiting rooms of various fertility clinics. My innate enthusiasm was tamped down, my bubbles, as my grandfather described them, had burst, popped on the jagged edges of life. In place of the work I was once so proud to share, there was now only shame. I had promised to keep it in the family; I hadn't. Four generations of shared passion and commitment would end with me.

What would my grandfather make of me, of the person I'd become? The girl he had adored, full of color and promise, had somehow flattened into an image I wasn't sure he'd recognize. I remembered our last dinner out together in the city, my grandparents and I around a table at the National Arts Club, my grandmother, as was customary, instructing my grandfather to order something laughably healthy ("Bill, you'll have the vegetables, it'll be good for you,") while she and I indulged in lobster. But he didn't care. He was too busy explaining a Spanish word to me, which loosely translated as that intangible, compelling quality; the "it" factor. To illustrate his point, he started rattling off examples. "Marilyn Monroe, she had it. Frank Sinatra had it. Derek Jeter's got it. It's that special something, and *you*, Amy, you have it, too."

Worse than losing myself, worse than losing whatever degree of "it" I'd ever had, was losing the piece I could never get back; the me that he loved. The me that was his. It made my grandfather feel farther away than he'd ever been—my palpable, pulsing memories, my keenly alive sense of him, all now trapped under glass.

## VOLUME II

The loss of my grandfather was the thing to make me feel true conviction about having children. Though it makes sense, I suppose, for death to be the thing that inspired me to try and create life, experiencing an urgent desire for children in that moment caught me off guard. But when he died, I realized that no matter how much time passed, no matter how long gone, he would forever be one of the most important people in my life. Next to him, among the very few others, were our future children. So in the days after his funeral, as impossible as it seemed that I would never see him again, I began to think about how my one-day children were still out there, somewhere in the future, waiting to be known and loved. I couldn't get back the love I had lost, but I could do my best to create more of it.

I guess you could say that it was grief that launched my quest for a baby. What I hadn't bargained for was that grief would continue to follow me like a looming shadow, hot on my heels, as I mourned the tangible losses (years, career, body parts, babies) and the intangibles (sanity, control, hope, normalcy). I felt the grief of every imagined child that was not to be many times over, an enduring anguish of weekly, monthly, yearly losses. Sometimes grief was quiet and listless, hunching my shoulders and bowing my head against the swirling leaves of late autumn, conducting a symphony of sadness through my earbuds as the wind carried me to yet another acupuncture appointment. Other times grief boiled, stealing my breath so that I gasped and my lungs heaved, desperate for air, its nails clawing beneath the neckline of my shirt, leaving my skin hot and blotchy after getting news of the latest delay in treatment. It was grief as an existence. Normalized grief.

And still, in a way, I was spared. In all my years of trying and failing to have a baby—three years total—I never suffered a traditional miscarriage. All my pregnancy losses were biochemical. Technically they were miscarriages, sure, but the earliest ones, the ones I discovered nine or so days after the embryo transfer during rounds of IVF. Each was communicated to me in a technical way—I'd had a positive blood test but was showing very low levels of hCG (human chorionic gonadotropin, the pregnancy hormone). That meant the pregnancy was clearly not viable. No one said the word *miscarriage.* There was a decency to the way my hope was extinguished—swiftly and completely and always by phone. I would hold my breath until I'd hung up with the nurse, then the sobs would explode, reverberating off the walls, shaking the room. Eventually, the roar gave way to a dull, ringing silence. Sometimes, I fell asleep. In time, my survival instinct would kick in and I'd immediately start to think about what we'd do next—how soon we could start another round of IVF. Getting a clear *no* caused me to suffer, no doubt, but at least it was quick and I could then move on.

I wondered, though, about the people who received good news, only to have it days later, or maybe weeks or even months later, become bad news. What was it like if hope was allowed to live, given oxygen so the flame could catch, allowed time to spread. What if hope had the chance to dance dangerously, to light up your world, before it burned down everything around you?

Our fourth round of IVF appeared to be another biochemical failure. My initial hCG count was 19—far below the 50-or-higher my doctor said we'd expect to see at this stage of a healthy pregnancy. It had been the first round with our new doctor, at our new clinic, and things had seemed so promising. We got the results four days after Christmas, took the afternoon to collect ourselves, then flew to Florida to see Tim's family for the holidays. On New Year's Eve we pulled into a Quest Diagnostics in a nearby strip mall so I could get some blood work done. We had to trace the hCG until it reached zero, until the glimmer of life was no more.

Only this time, the number rose. More than doubled, in fact, as though a healthy pregnancy was taking hold. The nurse who called me with the news sounded as surprised as I felt. Keep taking the progesterone shots, she told me. And go back to Quest for more blood work. As much as I willed myself to repress it, a hopeful smile crept to my lips. Don't get excited, my doctor cautioned, talking me through the results on a call from his holiday vacation spot to mine. It was January 2nd, the beginning of a year everyone felt sure would turn things around for us, what so many well-meaning friends and family members were insisting would be Our Year.

My doctor put the chance that this was a healthy baby at .01%. Extremely low odds, he said, because healthy babies just don't start below that threshold of 50. But the next blood draw was higher still, then higher again after that. Back in New York the following week, my doctor couldn't explain the increases, but he had upped the odds to .1%. "Listen," he told me. "Have there ever been real, live babies born that started out with low hCGs? Absolutely. Is it likely? No." But he went on to speculate, optimistically, that the pregnancy could be viable but had just implanted late. Or maybe it was an ectopic pregnancy—the worst-case scenario. If it was, if the embryo had implanted and started growing outside my uterus, I would either need emergency surgery to remove it or I would have to take a drug that would prevent us from trying again for three months. A huge setback either way.

The next night a hollow, unfamiliar pain reverberated across my stomach and pelvis. I described it as cramps only because I didn't have a better word. I shifted endlessly on the couch trying to get comfortable and could barely sit to eat dinner. Hours later, the pain woke me from sleep. Early the next morning, as my doctor performed an ultrasound, the room was silent. When he eventually spoke, he said I needed to go straight to the Emergency Room.

Apparently, my abdomen was full of fluid, possibly (dangerously) blood, possibly (more innocently) from a sac left behind by one of the eggs that had been retrieved a few weeks earlier. It looked like an ectopic pregnancy on the ultrasound but would need to be viewed on the hospital's more sensitive equipment before we could know for sure.

Waiting to be seen in the ER, I played the part of a calm, easygoing person, sending Jessie a happy birthday email, then texting Desi to cancel our dinner plans that night. I thought about how I wished I had showered or put on deodorant before I left the house. I told Tim not to come yet, not until we knew definitively what was going on.

"Ok, let's see," a nurse said, looking down at the intake forms. "How far along are you?"

"Oh, I'm not actually pregnant," I explained too quickly, determined not to let her get the wrong idea. "It was an IVF cycle, the date of my embryo transfer was December 18th, but it's not a viable pregnancy. My doctor saw free fluid this morning and he thinks it's an ectopic but isn't positive."

They ran blood tests and did a vaginal exam. "You're five weeks and four days pregnant," the resident reported, clear and clipped, as one line from the chart in her hands exploded off the page: **Due September 6th**.

The impact was immediate. I had never had a due date. Not this cycle, nor any of the ones that came before it.

Awaiting more tests, I lay in a hospital bed in the hallway of the ER for hours that day, blood pooling in my abdominal cavity (as was later confirmed), and thought about that due date. *My* due date. So matter of fact, a fundamental truth. A single, arbitrary day on the calendar and suddenly this person had shape, like one of those tiny capsules I had played with growing up, those little balls of nothing that spring into their foam selves when fully submerged. This person, this tiny person—was real. Was trying to live. This baby's cells were multiplying. This baby didn't want to let go.

A nurse named Caroline took care of me that day. She was kind in a casual way, not overly chipper, but relaxed and pleasant. When I left the house that morning, I thought I'd be right back, just out for a quick blood draw before returning home for breakfast, so I hadn't eaten anything since the night before. In the ER I wasn't allowed food or water and with each passing hour I more acutely felt the flush of my cheeks, the throb of my head. At some point in the afternoon Caroline approached in her unhurried way to see how I was doing. "I'm ok," I said, trying to adopt her offhandedness. "Just thirsty." "Let me see if I can get you some ice chips," she offered. "That shouldn't be a problem." By my estimation Caroline and I were about the same age, and her gesture of ice chips, which registered as a supreme kindness, confirmed my suspicion that we were officially ER best friends.

There was terrible cell reception in that part of the hospital, so my doctor and I spent hours struggling to reach each other. His repeated calls to me wouldn't go through, so eventually a resident walked over with a phone so we could speak. My blood work and ultrasound results were still inconclusive, he explained, so we had three options; I could go home, though he said he was reluctant to allow that; I could stay overnight for observation, waiting a little longer to suss out a definitive diagnosis; or I could go in for exploratory surgery, at which point they would be able to identify and fix whatever it was that had gone awry. "You don't have to decide right now," he said. "Talk to Tim. Let's speak again in a bit to come up with a plan."

The ER was at capacity, so my bed remained in the hallway, pushed up against the nurse's station. A patient in a paper gown staggered out from somewhere and began spewing loud, intense anger at the hospital staff, prompting a brief cease in the steady hum of operations as several people tried to calm her down. I got the sense they all knew her well enough. It was stuffy and windowless down there, with heat churning out of dust-lined vents, and when I finally caught sight of myself in the bathroom mirror there were circles of pink patched across my cheeks. I grabbed a stack of paper towels and held it under the sink before dragging the wet clump back and forth under my armpits. I wondered if my body odor was powerful enough that my friend Caroline had noticed.

Eventually, I told Tim to come and late that afternoon he arrived in a flurry of confusion and worry. I reassured him that everything was fine, and we debated my three options. In the end, though, the decision was made for us; an expert gyn radiologist was ultimately the one to diagnose the ectopic pregnancy in my right fallopian tube. As soon as an operating room became available, I was wheeled up for surgery. After a full day of waiting and uncertainty, things suddenly unfolded swiftly; my doctor hurried into the ER, down jacket over his scrubs, scarf trailing behind him, so he could be the one to cut me open; I scribbled my signature on some paperwork, and he pushed me himself through the tired hallways.

It was close to midnight when I left the hospital—without an embryo, without a fallopian tube, without a due date—and the words continued to haunt me.

*5 weeks, 4 days*

*Due September 6th*

Those words, that due date were, for me, the difference between a failed cycle and the loss of a baby. Who would he have been, I wondered, this tiny person I felt sure was a little boy. I could only imagine his face, his laugh, his gifts. Maybe his eyes would have twinkled, as my grandfather's did. If only he had burrowed a few centimeters in a different direction. The difference couldn't have been more than a few centimeters.

After the surgery, everything hurt. My throat was raw from the breathing tube, my abdomen throbbed, my heart ached. Officially, I had lost an organ, a fallopian tube I no longer needed since we weren't getting pregnant the regular way. That's what I said when I recounted the story of that crazy day, but I always left out a lone detail—the fact that come September, I was supposed to have a baby. That I had lost a son. Only there was no funeral to attend, no familiar ritual to help me make sense of my grief, no other mourners to share the weight of my sorrow. Tim was focused on my health, my recovery. He didn't absorb the loss as I did, as the absence of something—of some*one*—who had been there, and then wasn't. I was the only person who seemed aware of what had happened, walking around, dimmed almost beyond recognition, numbly going about my life. I had dinner with friends, sat through a baby shower. Back at home, I gasped for air.

I did think about ways Tim and I could honor that little baby, a small ceremonial moment in nature, just to acknowledge that he had once been here. I imagined us near a lake, setting something down and watching it float away, the water carrying and cradling it until it was entirely out of sight. But then life marched on, the future pulling us toward yet another surgery, more IVF, the next round of loss. With nowhere else to go, the grief stitched itself into me, its jagged edges smoothing over time, like the brownish scars I now carry, etched about an inch in from each of my pubic bones. Little wings. The one on my right side is darker and longer, marking the place where a tube and a baby once lived. But I don't need a scar to remember. How could I ever forget?

# Love

***

My toes were pointed skyward, the backs of my calves and thighs grazing the length of the headboard until they reached my butt, which was perched at the top of the bed where a pillow would normally be. This was the ritual. In our dark Brooklyn bedroom, ambient city lights glowing out the window, an above-ground subway rattling over the tracks in the distance, there were four bare feet suspended in mid-air. We formed two parallel human Ls, Tim and I, side by side in inverted repose, chatting as we called upon the force of gravity to help us make a baby. In the early days, when we were still having sex to try to get pregnant, this methodology had come to our attention; that 20 or 30 minutes of laying this way after sex would improve the odds of his sperm finding my egg. It might have been logical, implausible, or utterly ridiculous—I still can't decide.

*Alright*, I'd say breathlessly, my heart thumping, *legs are going up!* To his credit, Tim almost always joined me, swiveling 180 degrees, scootching his butt toward the top of the mattress, extending his legs as far as they'd go. He was game to keep me company, to look a fool alongside me, never balking at the rather abrupt transition from the lustful to the ludicrous.

The practice required absolute unselfconsciousness. We had to be willing not only to expose our stripped-down selves, but to be laughably naked—parts flipped at odd angles, nudity rendered absurd. If there is a word that can be defined as the *opposite of sexy*, that was us. Had it just been me, Tim lying right as rain checking emails while I cirque du soleil-ed it, I might have felt irritated, resentful. But with a partner in this nonsense, walking our four feet skyward, I felt a kind of electric closeness. In many ways, this part was more intimate than the sex itself.

Plus, it's tough to be guarded or to take yourself too seriously while laying naked and upside down. On those nights we were our freest selves, the words coming out in an easy tumble, as if the forces of gravity were at play there too. When the tone was light and laughing, we discussed the details of our days or grabbed an iPhone to play a song one of us wanted to share. In more serious moods we'd talk baby names, or fears about how it was going, where we might be headed. I'd fix my gaze ahead, entertained by the shadows performing a pas de deux on the ceiling, and find words I wasn't brave enough to utter in the light of day, the *what ifs*.

That's not to say I wasn't watching the clock. When my heels first touched the headboard, my body still warm, a spritz of sweat across my forehead, I made a point to note the time. I was committed to staying put for 30 minutes, the complete duration, no matter how late it was or how exhausted I felt. As the minutes passed and heat escaped my skin, I'd pull the covers taut around me, maybe poke my phone for a time check. Some nights, if there was a lull in conversation, I'd hear Tim's breathing grow steady, his mouth emitting a rhythmic whistle, then turn my head for confirmation. It always felt unjust that he was free to pass out at any time, good sport though he was. Why was it my responsibility to make it to the finish line? Sometimes, I'd shoot him some side eye, offering an exasperated sigh to the cold, quiet room, then resume the point/flex/point/flex of my airborne feet, turning a critical gaze to the bulge of my bunions, or assess how badly I needed a pedicure, until my phone let me off the hook.

Tim and me, upside down, two right angles, was how we got this thing started. We contorted ourselves first, and soon enough everything else—our life, our marriage—was turned on its head too. Once they travel through infertility, all the familiar images of love and affection become inverted, refracted, multiplied, splayed out, repeated at odd angles in perpetuity. The composition may be recognizable, retaining its colors, its saturation, but the rearrangement leads to something new. A bizarre, beautiful mess.

\*\*\*

*I love being married to you, I love our adventures together, I love the moment when you walk in the door every night, I love the journey we are on—ups, downs, wins, challenges—because it is* **ours**, *I love that you are truly my best friend, as weird as it sounds I love driving over the Brooklyn Bridge and up the FDR to the fertility doctor with you, I love that we are a two-person family and I love the hope that we will someday add more into the mix. I just love being next to you, and everything that happens is deeper, richer, less difficult or more wonderful because you are there with me. Thank you for choosing to marry me. Three years in, I love you more than ever. (Card written to Tim, September 17, 2014)*

\*\*\*

The kitchen was where I started pulling down my pants every morning, challenging our already lowered standards of sexiness, to say nothing of the breach of hygiene norms. It was there, within spitting distance of a pantry lined with rice and flour and cans of beans, where we created our makeshift medical hub. The logic was that since certain drug vials required refrigeration, shooting up in the kitchen made the most sense.

When the meds first arrived, I rummaged around our apartment for some sort of receptacle, then settled on the least-sterile bin I could find: a large, rectangular box made of a natural, woven material that looked like straw but probably wasn't. Inside, I arranged everything with precision, adamant that I would make order out of chaos, ensure our at-home fertility hub excelled at such things as tidiness and proximity to snacks. In the right angle of one corner I tucked the red biomedical waste bin, followed by a plastic bag stuffed with syringes, then boxes of bandages and alcohol swabs, with medication vials fanning out from there. We lived in a loft-style building, an old water meter factory converted into apartments, and the kitchen was part of a large open living space that included our dining table, couch, and TV. That meant that from virtually any angle, no matter what we were doing, the box was in our line of sight, as essential to survival as food itself.

Once I was no longer working, Tim, who rose in the dark to shower and dress for a day at the office, became my alarm clock, rustling me before he left, letting me know it was time to meet in the kitchen. I'd loaf sleepily behind him, wash my hands, robotically fill a syringe, and run my fingers behind me, beneath the waist of my sweatpants, searching for a bandage glued to my flesh. The morning progesterone shots pierce the muscle of the upper outer corner of the butt cheek, on alternate sides each day. Once I knew where the last shot had gone and this latest one belonged, I'd drop trou.

The scene in our kitchen was unbalanced, discordant. Needles where there should have been spoons, glass vials the size of a human thumb in place of cereal bowls steaming with oatmeal. Tim, hair damp from the shower, notes of cologne clinging to the starched collar of his shirt, and me, my teeth shrink-wrapped in morning film, my underwear and stretched-out sweatpants lowered to expose droopy, dimpled skin dotted with bruises.

As I curled fingers around the edge of the countertop, bracing for the needle, I could see my butt in my mind's eye, as seen by Tim. Pale, limp gooseflesh. The word *flaccid* comes to mind. This, for the most part, had become the extent of Tim's exposure to my body. We weren't supposed to have sex during IVF, so as not to interfere with the growth of eggs, or the implantation of an embryo. This unceremonious pants-dropping, my naked, bruised butt in broad daylight, against the backdrop of a dirty microwave, was what it had come to.

Objectively, I was aware that the entire exercise was humiliating. Tim right behind me, handsome and put together and accomplished, and me at my saddest, most unappealing. I could see and understand it all clearly when I stepped outside of myself and looked down from above. Yet it was the absence of sentiment that struck me most. The scene might read humiliating, but I did not feel humiliated. My thinking brain and my emotional brain were in firm disagreement.

"Ok," I'd say, twisting my head and peering down over a shoulder, jabbing my pointer finger into my butt. "Riiight here."

Tim would then poke with his own finger, confirming the target. "Here?"

"No," I corrected him, "here." Every day there seemed to be one precise place where the shot belonged. I felt it with great conviction.

"Isn't that what I just said? Anyway, I've got it." He swirled an alcohol swab over the area. "Ready? One…two…three."

And then it was done. I'd feel the muscle under my flesh seize, then quickly unclench, easing into a gentle throb. Some days a dot of blood would ball where the needle had entered, and Tim would use a cotton swab to blot it before applying the bandage. If no red appeared, he'd congratulate himself on a clean injection, disproportionately pleased with his medical acumen.

"No blood today! Not bad, you've gotta give it to me, I'm getting good," he'd say with a smile, before kissing me goodbye. "Ok, I gotta go. I love you."

"Love you too," I'd call, re-knotting the tie of my sweatpants.

Then he'd leave, hurrying toward the subway, and I would walk myself across the room and flop on the couch, a tiny fire raging inside the skin beneath me.

***

*I really am sorry for snapping on Sunday morning; as I was walking downstairs my eyes were tearing up and I just felt this intense anger and sadness. I think I have sort of tried to keep it all in and search for solutions, but then at the same time I reach a point and just crack. I don't want our life to be waking up for shots, being terrified of the bad news, not being able to plan things, both being unhappy at work! It just feels endless, and I really do try and stay positive, but sometimes I lose it. For whatever reason it sort of helps me to yell and get angry, but I realize it is not productive and also just stressful for you. The last thing I want to do is make it any harder for you. (Email from Tim, October 2014)*

***

Tim frequently worked late, so he'd arrive home to the lights already off, my silhouette on the couch flashing in fits and starts opposite a glowing TV. Certain shows we'd committed to watching together; these days it was *Parenthood* and *Breaking Bad*, an unlikely balm delivered via meth-lab-bleakness-meets-heartwarming-family-drama. Depending on the day, we might be pulled toward Walter White and his progression into darkness, the inner turmoil of Jesse Pinkman, all of it a complex and gripping acknowledgment of the cruelest aspects of this world. Or perhaps we'd opt for the Braverman clan, depicted in the opening credits as laughing and raising their glasses around a long outdoor table under a string of white lights, the notes of Bob Dylan's "Forever Young" casting the faded glow of nostalgia.

Those were the shows we'd take in side-by-side, our Friday and Saturday night escape. But when I was alone, my programming preferences took me in a different direction. On this evening, Tim crossed the room toward me and perched on the edge of the couch, his mouth cracking into a smile as his eyes took in the images on TV. "Let me guess," he ventured jauntily, "she lit up a room?"

If you've watched even a small sampling of *Dateline* episodes, you've surely heard this phrase used to describe a victim. It's often the first thing we learn about the person, who—predictably, disturbingly—is almost always a woman. *She was a bright light,* Keith Morrison's unmistakable voice begins, his delivery alternately halting and hurried, the nothing-to-see-here intonation he uses to render every pull-the-rug-out moment more effective. *She was so full of life. She lit up a room.* It's an important characterization up front, so that we can more fully appreciate the darkness of her death. Hers, we should understand, was a light extinguished. Tim despises *Dateline.* He'd prefer to watch *The Real Housewives* or *The Bachelor,* or possibly even the sale of limited-time-only sweater sets on QVC. But after sitting through countless episodes with me, he's gotten a handle on how the show works.

"She sure did light up a room," I confirmed. "And her husband, you'll be shocked to learn, is an absolute psychopath."

"Ooh, don't tell me—he took out life insurance on her?" Tim shot back.

I smiled. This is another hallmark of *Dateline* mysteries, an inordinate number of cases revolve around a life insurance policy that has been taken out on a spouse, sometimes mere days before she's killed. We're often led to suspect the husband but left wondering at the motive, and then, boom; we find out he took out a policy on her, and it all makes sense. She's out of the picture *and* he gets to collect a whole bunch of cash. If you are deranged and murderous, that is an unequivocal win/win.

"I'll tell you what," I said, "if you ever even *think* about taking out life insurance on me, I'll be gone so fast your head will spin."

Tim was grinning. "Oh, I meant to tell you, I actually did plan to take out a policy on you, I think I have to for work or something? But don't worry, I'd only collect, like, 10 million dollars if something were to happen to you."

"Oh, ok, cool," I said laughing, "well in that case."

We sat back and watched for a bit.

"At least in this one it wasn't an oxygen tank, I just cannot make sense of why so many women are willing to go scuba diving with their husbands when they are having serious marital problems," my voice cut through the dark room. "Does no one see that he's going to remove your air supply and make it look like an accident? And there will be no witnesses under water? I will literally never agree to go scuba diving with you."

"Well, obviously I'd never do anything so predictable," Tim said playfully, his eyes dancing with amusement. "As you know, I've already planned the perfect murder."

"Ah, yes," I said, "your ingenious plot."

"I mean, it's foolproof," Tim said with comical pride, before regaling me with his well-practiced spiel. "So it's the week of Thanksgiving," he began, "and I go to the store to buy a frozen turkey. Completely normal, right? But what no one realizes is that a frozen-solid turkey is also a blunt force object, the perfect tool to have on hand if you are looking to bludgeon someone. And that is where the true genius of it all lies; I kill you with the turkey, and then I *cook* the turkey. There's no murder weapon, because I've *eaten* it. And it's a long weekend, so I will have days and days before anyone even realizes that something has happened. And even then, I've done nothing suspicious! Sure, I'm on security footage at the grocery store buying a frozen turkey, but so is everyone else—it's Thanksgiving!"

"Wow," I said, smiling broadly, "the amount of thought you've put into this is seriously disturbing. I mean it's good, but there are definitely some holes. First of all, are you really going to be able to sit alone and eat an entire turkey after you've used it to kill me? Also, you would have to dispose of my body, and I think our families would have questions about why we weren't spending the holiday with them. But, sure. There's potential."

"Potential?!" he said with exaggerated disbelief. "What I'm hearing is some jealousy that you didn't think of it yourself. Regardless, Thanksgiving is coming up, so if I were you, I'd keep your head on a swivel."

I laughed, and rolled my eyes, and felt grateful for the humor between us, macabre or otherwise. It was the thing keeping me afloat.

That year, I not only made it through another Thanksgiving (phew!), but found a special gift from Tim beneath the Christmas tree. It was not a life insurance policy (also phew!), but a very cozy *Dateline* Snuggie.

\*\*\*

*I know you feel so alone but you always have me. We are in this together and we will get through it together. My sister keeps reminding me of this quote:* **in the end, everything will be ok. And if it's not ok, then it's not the end.** *We don't know what is going to happen, but we are going to keep pushing. We are going to get there. (Email to Tim, October 2014).*

\*\*\*

On weeknights, it was not unusual for me to eat dinner without Tim. Occasionally I'd order takeout for myself, assuming he would have something at work, and watch *Jeopardy!* in the living room with feet propped on the coffee table, plate in my lap. Other times I cooked, healthy fare that might help massage my organs, convince them to finally start functioning properly. I'd whip up clear broth a la Gwyneth, with chicken and greens, or quinoa studded with roasted squash, or sautéed leeks. I'd eat alone but save some for Tim, in case he was hungry when he arrived.

On this particular night, the ground was covered with slick yellow leaves, wet from the October rain and illuminated by the glare of headlights and street lamps. Tim walked in the door long after I'd finished my meal. "There's food if you want some," I told him, after we'd said hello. "Thanks," he said. "I haven't eaten yet. I actually left work a while ago." There was a pause. "I went to light a candle." His words sounded strange, unfamiliar. I looked up slowly. Muted the TV. "You lit a candle?" "Yeah. I walked to St. Patrick's and lit a candle. I needed to think and I needed to do something and I don't know. It just felt right."

We were awaiting the results of our third round of IVF, and Tim, especially, was suffering. The lack of control, the lack of answers, the overwhelming stress. I had been encouraging him to try therapy, or acupuncture, or start running more—all the things that had been keeping me somewhat sane. He had shrugged off my suggestions, and I hadn't realized he might privately be weighing some ideas of his own.

It should be said that I am not a religious person. My parents had me baptized as a baby, under an oak in our front yard, but never once took me to church. Not on Christmas, or Easter—never. It's funny, though, because religion as an ideal, as something fundamental to the existence of so many people on this planet, has in many ways shaped my identity. If a devout commitment to knowing God can be a defining factor in a person's life, so too can its absence.

My parents scarcely acknowledged religion at home; I wasn't taught to see it as bad, or good, or anything at all. As kids, my sister and I were curious about the Methodist church friends of ours attended, so we implored our parents to let us tag along. *Why not*, they shrugged, though they had no intention of bringing us themselves. So, on Sunday mornings we'd pull on a skirt and dash outside when our friends' parents turned their Subaru into our driveway, eager to accompany a family that wasn't ours to a church to which we did not belong.

Reflecting back, I see how brave we were, how curious, how powerful the need we must have felt to be a part of something bigger. I picture us there just as the sermon let out, two unclaimed kids at waist-level amidst an unfamiliar congregation, weaving through the crowd to swipe a couple of cookies before Sunday School. The echo-y hallways, the worksheets summarizing Biblical tales, moving our mouths along aimlessly when everybody recited prayers in unison, the sense that everyone knew so much more than we did.

The majority of our town was of Catholic faith, so in middle school a big group would meet outside after dismissal on Tuesday afternoons to walk together to CCD, the religious education program of the Catholic Church. All the kids complained about it, but I would have given anything to join them. A group who had in common this significant foundational experience, who were united in this higher calling of which I knew nothing. Somewhere along the way, I had internalized the notion that to be religious was to be the right sort of person. Decent. Virtuous. Better. Without faith on my side, I understood that I had more to prove. I'd have to do everything right, be moral, kind, and hardworking to the greatest extent possible.

It can only be seen as an act of self-punishment, then, that I chose to attend a Catholic college, joining a student body for whom religion was an essential piece of daily life. We'd all party together over the weekend, then, as dusk blanketed campus on Sunday evening, groups of 19 and 20-year-olds would head out for mass while I hung back in the dorm, my solitary presence a pronouncement of Otherness. It's perverse, really. Why would I have chosen that? What possessed me to seek out a place where, at least in this one sense, I wouldn't belong? I suppose that while religion is not a part of my life, faith is still something that *matters* to me, in ways I'm still trying to figure out. I respect its tenets, admire its ideals, long for the comfort it offers. Perhaps positing myself near people of faith, living and studying among them, befriending them, even marrying one of them, has been my own way of discovering the truth of what I believe. Faith was not handed to me, so I've set out to find it for myself.

Tim is a Catholic, he was one of those people in college who found himself in a church pew most Sunday nights. I didn't know him back then, and in the time since his faith had grown quieter, less overt; he hadn't attended mass in all the years I'd known him. To hear, now, that he'd sat quietly in the back of a church praying, met God in a space of worship, lit a candle and asked for holy assistance—the idea alone was radical enough to reverberate through my entire being. Tim's burning candle, his personal appeal flickering in St. Patrick's at that very moment, struck me with its own sort of divine power.

"How did it feel?" I asked, with genuine wonder.

"It was good," he said simply. "I'm glad I went."

"That's really great," I offered, hoping he could tell just how much I meant it. "Thank you for doing that."

\*\*\*

*We have this amazing thing together and yet we don't get to spend enough time with just us and even when we do we are so focused on IVF that we can't relax … We just have to keep pushing forward and pray for the best … I do know I have you and we have us and that makes me smile so much and gives me a sense of comfort. You are the best thing in my world, and I have no clue what I would do without you. (Email from Tim, October 2014)*

\*\*\*

An embryo transfer takes no time at all. Once your thick hospital socks plod across the cold vinyl of the exam room and you make your way onto the table, there are maybe a handful of minutes left. A quick visit from an embryologist to confirm that your name and date of birth match those on the glass vial in her hands, and it's go-time, the whole shebang a far cry from giggling as you climb your legs up the wall. Here, I was an island in the center of a cold, gleaming sea of equipment. Here, I spread my feet in opposite directions, like two magnets repelling each other, until they found their respective stirrups.

Beneath a metal spotlight I'd lay back, stiff paper gown crinkling beneath me, and think the same thought every time; how strange that Tim isn't even in the room for this baby's conception. It was one thing for us not to get pregnant naturally, but it felt outrageously wrong for him to not even be in the *room*. This was illogical, of course. The truth is that neither of us had been in the room. His sperm and my egg had already fused, in an embryology lab months earlier, before being frozen and stored for a future transfer. For all I knew that potential child of ours had been made while we were on the couch together, Tim outlining the specifics of his plan to bludgeon me with a Thanksgiving turkey.

But it gnawed at me, Tim not being there. It wasn't that I wanted any kind of support from him, just his presence. For the symbolism. He should have been in the room. Since that wasn't permitted, I tried to think of him. Keep him contained and vivid in my consciousness, so that, to whatever extent the intangible mattered, he would be there in some way too.

If I'd had more time on that exam table, I'd have let my mind wander, tracing the details of any number of memories, like the birthday, back when I was still at my magazine job, when Tim took the subway to my office instead of his, walked into the Starbucks I visited on my way into work each day, paid for my coffee, then continued on to his own job. When I got to the counter that morning, the barista smiled and said, "It's already paid for. Your boyfriend was here. Happy birthday." Or maybe I would have recalled our time living in Boston, where I'd sit cradled in the front alcove of our apartment, my desk pushed up against the picture window, Tim returning home each day from business school, pedaling his bike through the afternoon light. Seeing his face appear on our empty cobblestone street, his broad smile, the way he threw his arm up into the air to wave at me through the window; I will never forget the sight of it, or how it made me feel.

Throughout infertility, when the world seemed to be telling us that we were not meant to have a baby, I often fixated on the notion that maybe this love, Tim and me, was enough. What we had found in each other—partnership, challenge, a person who brought out our respective best selves—was what life was all about, and how could I dare to ask for more than that? I was lucky. No matter what else happened, I was truly lucky.

Had there been more time to spend on that examining room table, I might have let my mind revisit any one of a million tiny moments. Instead, the procedure was over in an instant, and all I had time to think of was his name. "Ok, Amy, hold still, you may feel a bit of pressure." I stared up at the ceiling, cold and cavernous. *Tim. Tim. Tim.* Forcing him into the room with me. Fixated on the word. Not the man. Not the love. "Ok, that's it. It's in there. Here's a picture of the embryo; good luck to you."

# Loneliness

***

Holding hands beneath the table has always been our thing, Stephanie and me. Not a lacing of fingers exactly, more like a loose clasp swinging back and forth, or a comforting patting of palms. We even play a game, if you can call it that, in which we rotate our wrists so that our joined hands flip repeatedly, alternating whose is on top, while singing like two silly children, "everybody wins, nobody loses." We are two sisters for whom all thumb wars lead to peace.

The handholding might have started when we were little girls, when I was two and Stephanie was six perhaps, but we continued the tradition into adulthood, two women in their 20s, 30s, and then 40s, holding hands beneath the dinner table, on holidays and birthdays, or any other time the family gathers. Maybe we got it from our mom, who, when we were children in the back of our parents' Buick, would often reach her arm up and over the head rest so that it dangled behind the passenger seat, where she'd open and shut her hand a couple of times, code for one of us to grab it. She did this when we were upset, or if we'd gotten in trouble and the mood in the car was tense; a mother's comfort extended through this wordless, faceless gesture. Sometimes she did it for no reason at all, simply because an outstretched palm looks like love.

It's telling, in a way, because our mom was always there but we could never really *see* her. She would tell you she is a private person, we would say she is all but inaccessible, even to her daughters. She was willing to sit atop our comforters and read an entire stack of books at bedtime, but when asked directly for an innocuous story from her own life—*where did you go on vacation as a kid? Who were your friends in high school?*—she wasn't willing to provide an answer. Just a long pause and a *let me think about it and get back to you.* When I've attempted to reach her, looking for support or guidance with friend issues in middle school or boy angst later on, she would listen, but not be able to connect in a meaningful way. Instead, I would get a blanket reassurance; *not to worry, it will all be OK.* Feeling unheard, I'd contract once again, silenced by a renewed awareness that my mother and I speak two different languages.

As kids we would visit our grandmother in the house my mom grew up in, digging up old scrapbooks and photo albums from the '60s to try to get to know her, piecing together clues and conjuring up our own theories to fill in the holes. To this day, my sister is as drawn to mysteries as I am; perhaps it is the mystery of our mom, whom we've spent decades trying to solve, that started it all. Who did she hang out with in college, we wondered, what were the names of her old boyfriends? We learned she was a cheerleader and a member of a sorority, and one day there was a dramatic break in the case when we discovered her arrest for stealing a stop sign as a teenager (our tote-bag-carrying, recycling-enthusiast mom—*behind bars?!*). She had all the makings of a perfect mystery. Who was she, really? What sort of person had she been? Who was she now? What heartaches and achievements and milestones had lodged themselves inside of her? We ached for the answers.

We both knew our mom would do anything for us—a more selfless person does not exist. But maybe that's the thing, we craved *more* of her self, not less. How could we ever fully know ourselves, after all, if we couldn't know the person from whom we came? Besides, it's hard to feel close to someone so sealed off, so prone to shutting down our questions with awkward deflections. How could we open up ourselves, allow our own vulnerability, when she offered us no way in?

Perhaps it wasn't surprising, then, that Stephanie and I came to speak a language of our own, one born of mutual need. We communicate through our joined hands, fluttering fingers to indicate excitement, giving a prolonged squeeze when our parents say or do something particularly irritating. She is a social worker, I am a writer, and together we are two highly sensitive sisters who shared a childhood that was more, shall I say, offbeat than most. Our mom on the front step at dusk, ringing an antique bell to summon us in for dinner; settling in afterward to watch *The Patty Duke Show*, or *The Dick Van Dyke Show*, or any number of other black and white programs from the 1960s being re-aired on Nick at Nite. We grew up in the '80s and '90s without ever being exposed to the cult classic movies of our era (*Ferris Bueller's Day Off*, *National Lampoon's Christmas Vacation*). But we knew every word of every song from the Technicolor musicals *Singin' in the Rain* and *Meet Me in St. Louis*.

While my sister and I mostly had our own distinct interests— she played piano, I played soccer; she liked boys, I liked books— musicals were a shared source of joy. Through VHS tapes borrowed from the library we got an education in the classics: *The Music Man*, *My Fair Lady*, *South Pacific*. After school we'd play the soundtracks on repeat, belting the words as we gestured and twirled along. When I was six, our grandparents took us to see a Broadway show for the first time. Scarcely eye-level with the white tablecloth during dinner, I wore my fanciest dress, eventually taking my seat in the gilded theater, patent leather flats kicking back and forth above the floor.

As we sat waiting for the show to begin, I took in the unfamiliar strains of a live orchestra warming up, the distinct notes and phrases—the dense vibration of a bow grazing strings, a high-pitched flutter escaping a woodwind, together creating a sort of captivating discord. Finally, the noise quieted. The lights dimmed. Stephanie and I looked at each other then sat up straight. There seemed to be a single moment when every one of us in the theater was holding our breath, and then the instruments burst into their collective, exquisite magic.

That first show was *Me and My Girl*, and in the years that followed, we begged our parents to take us to Broadway whenever possible. When I turned 16, instead of wishing for a car, or a party, I asked to bring a few friends to see *Miss Saigon*. It was around then that my grandfather created a new tradition: for his birthday every year, all he wanted was the company of his family at a show. I remember hearing him speak about his days growing up in Queens, how as a boy he would travel into Manhattan to make some money sweeping the floors of the theaters. He was mesmerized by the lights and glamour and escape of it all, and while standing in an ornate lobby, whisking away dust and trash, he fantasized about the day when he'd walk in the door, present his ticket, and claim his own seat in the audience.

Seven decades later, it was a particular accomplishment to be able to bring his children and grandchildren—ten of us—for his birthday shows. We'd meet for dinner in the theater district, the same restaurant from all those years back, still covered wall-to-wall with caricatures of actors and musicians and athletes, before dispersing into the surrounding neighborhood, four to this show, another four to that one, two to still another—then meet back at the restaurant for dessert and reviews. Who saw what with whom varied from year to year, but it went without saying that the Gallo sisters stayed together, hands fluttering all the way.

*** 

Rushing into the city from Brooklyn, taking the C train to 50th street to meet my mom and sister and her daughter, Alexa, I'm pretty sure I was irritated before I even got there. It might have been the scramble that set me off, getting from point A to point B in New York City. Or it might have been my fertility meds. I had a few cycles of Clomid under my belt by that point and those can mess you up a bit, to say nothing of the stress of not getting pregnant in the first place. If I had to guess, though, my mood was due to a nagging knowledge in my subconscious, the anticipation of heading somewhere I didn't belong. "Veedie!" my sister exclaimed when she saw me. We've been calling each other "Veed" for so long it's hard to remember the original joke behind it, just one silly nickname in an extensive private lexicon. "Hi Veed," I said, as we gave each other a one-armed hug.

The occasion was a matinee of *Cinderella,* a new musical starring Carly Rae Jepsen. For Alexa, who was nearly seven, watching a pop star leading lady sing and dance her way through a fairy tale was about as good a day as she could hope to have. But first we were stopping at a retro diner where the wait staff belted show tunes into a microphone, spinning among the tables trying to rouse the crowd, occasionally hopping on top of booths for added entertainment. As a concept, I wholly endorsed this place; what's not to enjoy about a star-worthy soprano singing "Don't Rain on my Parade," before depositing a plate of French fries in front of you? There is simply not one thing wrong with that. Today, though, the entire atmosphere grated; I experienced it all as a lot of extra noise. "What shay you," my sister said, smiling. It's how we ask each other *how are you*, or *what's going on?* "Nothing, Veed," I replied, knowing that wasn't quite true but unable or unwilling to articulate what was. Instead, I directed my attention toward Alexa. "Are you excited?" My voice was raised a smidge too high. "It's gonna be so fun!"

The day Alexa was born, suddenly and surprisingly six weeks before we were expecting her, I felt an expansion in my heart, in my entire self. Being her aunt brings me extraordinary joy, and it's also something I do not take lightly; my sister is a single mom, and has been since Alexa was two, so my parents and I have all assumed our roles in her life with a greater sense of responsibility. In their early days as a two-person family, I commuted up from the city to sleep on their couch most Tuesday nights. My parents became regular caregivers, taking Alexa to swimming lessons, picking her up after school, hosting her and my sister for weekly dinners. We strive to be fun, in the way that grandparents and aunts should be, but none of us has ever lost sight of the fact that we are needed. In big ways sometimes, but often just by showing up—for performances of *The Nutcracker* at Christmastime, at Alexa's birthday parties, or the occasional matinee of *Annie* or *Cinderella*. So I did. Even as my childlessness had started to feel especially painful.

At the theater, an usher handed us our programs and pointed out our row. As I recall it, Stephanie and I did not sit beside each other, choosing instead to flank Alexa, with our mom down at the end. That we were separated was just as well; I was not in the mood for chit-chat or funny nicknames or even hand-holding. Instead, I leafed through my program, admired the scenery, and scanned the audience: the crowd was comprised, almost without exception, of mothers and daughters.

Except for me. Which I observed, and then, in the shadows of Act I, beneath the thump of an upbeat score, I felt. Ripples of laughter spreading from the orchestra section up through the mezzanine while I sat stone-faced; raucous applause while I politely tapped my hands. It was a feeling entirely at odds with what I had always found enchanting about being part of an audience; the hours-long connection with strangers. The experience of being lifted and moved and crushed in unison; the magic of laughing or cheering or shedding tears in the dark alongside people you've never met. Today, though, I was alone. The daughters were cupping hands over the earring-ed lobes above them so they could whisper this or that; the mothers were sneaking sideways glances down at their enraptured little faces. I was an intruder. Plainly, devastatingly so.

At intermission, Stephanie and Alexa squeezed down the row to find the bathroom, and my mom turned toward me. "What do you think?" she asked. "Isn't it *fun?*" I wish the relationship between us was such that I could have said, *I feel lonely. This is hard.* Instead, I ignored her question and released my pain in dagger form. "It's extremely hurtful to me that none of you come into the city to see me, but you have no problem making the trip to do these kinds of things," I said, gesturing around. "And you expect me to join, which is fine, I *want* to join, but we moved to Brooklyn eight months ago and you've never even seen our apartment." Stephanie and Alexa's jackets rested on the empty seats between us. There was a lot of space.

My mom was clearly caught off guard, but her face quickly widened in apology. "Amy, we want to see your apartment. I'm sorry we haven't been there and I'm sorry you feel hurt, I don't want you to feel that way." I stared out at the stage. I believed every word of what I was saying—*they live an hour away!* I often thought, outraged—but the real wound was the implication behind it: that I alone wasn't enough to warrant a visit. That my presence was expected everywhere, but my company wasn't worth the drive. If I'd had a baby for them to coo at, I thought bitterly, then surely they would have been knocking on my door.

I came at my mom that day because I couldn't come at my sister. I've never been able to tolerate fighting with Stephanie. Truthfully, there has rarely been reason to. We are both hardwired for empathy, and she is, without exception, the kindest, most caring person I have ever known. She has nurtured me my entire life; the person I call when I need to vent or laugh or feel understood or cared about; if I have a cold coming on or when I want someone to listen and tell me it's all going to be ok. Even the absurdity we engage in, the silly voices and handholding, informs the depth of our connection, facilitating a sort of wide-openness between us. We are unabashedly vulnerable with each other: it is our way of saying, here, you are safe.

Right now, though, I was angry. That she, too, hadn't visited me in Brooklyn, but more so because she knew about the Clomid, about the deepening struggle to have a baby, and yet it still hadn't occurred to her that today might be hard for me.

When they returned from the bathroom I looked up from my Playbill and smiled at Alexa, asking what she thought so far, which part she'd liked the best. I focused on her because she was the reason we were here, an almost-seven-year-old with a huge toothy grin and hearts on her sweater squealing about *Cinderella* and Carly Rae. As for Stephanie, we spoke briefly in plain English instead of our nonsensical sisters' dialect, which, frankly, said it all.

As we settled back in our seats and the lilt of orchestral notes invited us back into the story, I was immersed in a story of my own, incredulous that my sister hadn't read my mind. *How can she not see that I am all alone in this theater, that right now, I really need a hand?*

*\*\*\**

As I hurried from the train station to the restaurant, I dropped my chin to my chest, curling into myself to brace against the cold—and the company. I was going to a baby shower brunch for Jessie; most of our high school friends would be there, and I would be the only one of the group in attendance who didn't have a baby. But soon after we had all hugged and kissed hello, Jessie's friends at one end of a long table, her family at the other, it occurred to me that I was the only non-mother there, period. I kept track of these sorts of things and could perform an assessment with the quickest of tallies. *Her cousin has kids, yep, her boss does, too, and all the older women in her family. So yeah, that's everyone. It's just me.* I stared at my plate and adjusted my silverware, letting the thought settle.

Jessie was round and beaming, midway down the table. I was across and slightly diagonal from her, in a booth that ran the length of the wall, wedged into my seat by a handful of moms on either side. It had been only three weeks since the surgery to remove my ectopic pregnancy, and I felt pale and weary still. But here I was, talking babies and catching up with my friends, though I had little to contribute. Still, I surprised myself by feeling somewhat energized, simply by engaging with people I loved out in the world.

I'd last seen the girls around Christmas, when Tim and I had been awaiting the results of our IVF cycle, but only Jessie knew how it had all played out. Had we been anywhere else, under different circumstances, I would have shared it all unreservedly. Here, though, I wasn't sure I could do it without being wildly inappropriate. It's hard to imagine a less welcome baby shower topic than infertility (IBS? Identity theft? Chernobyl?).

It was Kaitlyn, I think, seated beside me, who discreetly asked how I was doing. We were angled toward each other, having a two-person conversation in low tones, and I spontaneously decided to answer her question with the truth: the rising hCG levels indicating a pregnancy, the confusion in the hospital when they couldn't see things clearly on the ultrasound, the ultimate ectopic diagnosis and emergency surgery to remove my fallopian tube. My voice was quiet, but it must have been the way we were speaking, the quiver of emotion, that made the others gradually cease their own speaking and start listening to me. I could feel eyes accumulating as I talked. *Wow*, someone said, once I had finished. *Oh my God, Amy. I can't believe it. Are you ok?*

There was a woman at the table, a friend of Jessie's from college whom I'd met a couple of times. She was something of an energy force field, and, seated directly across from me, her posturing and confidence made her the perfect foil for my bruised, shrunken shell. As a mom of three who had spent several years raising her kids abroad, she seemed to feel a particular kind of authority in this roomful of mothers. "Ugh, I completely get it," she projected to the table in response to having overheard some of my conversation with Kaitlyn. "My miscarriage was hell." It was how she said it—loudly, in a commanding sort of way, almost performative—that made it register as dismissive, even perversely one-upping, even though she probably thought she was commiserating. I nodded back at her, unable to speak, wishing I had one of those *People* magazines from the clinic to disappear behind, when I noticed Jessie listening in on the conversation as well.

The only thing worse than being the sad, infertile woman at the table was being the sad, infertile woman *talking* about being sad and infertile. I was mortified to have inadvertently presented my pain and struggles when we were all there for the purpose of celebrating a new life. Now it seemed like I was trying to distract from the real occasion, or to make things about me. One whole half of this shower, including Jessie, was in a grim discussion of my baby that would never be instead of hers who was nearly here. Check, please!

"*Anyway,*" I tried to smile at Jessie, to prove to her I was not sitting at her shower feeling sorry for myself, wrapped up in my own shit. Her eyes looked kind, full of understanding, as they so often did. "Does anyone have a strong feeling either way? Boy or girl?" It was my feeble attempt at a segue.

Before long Jessie was standing with her mom at the far end of the table, trying to maneuver around her tummy to open presents. I soon realized that the moms had largely overlooked the baby registry, and selected items that had proven invaluable in their own on-the-ground experience. The stuff you wouldn't know about unless you'd lived it. "My kids love these," Krissy said, as Jessie was unwrapping one adorable, baby-sized thing or another. "Oh yes, those are the best!" someone else chimed in. "So funny, I almost got you that too!" "I mean, it honestly wouldn't hurt to have two, I'd still get a second one if you can." They were gifting their wisdom, disguised as presents, while I had pointed and clicked through the registry, no hard-earned wisdom to give.

As the shower wound down, I found myself in receipt of a series of extra-tight hugs goodbye. Krissy offered to drive me to the train station, even though it couldn't have been more than a three-minute walk, and I gladly accepted. I sent a couple of texts from the platform to Tara, the third member of 7C, to say how much I'd missed her, and to Tim to let him know what time I'd be home, feeling a sort of hollow exhaustion, somehow even paler and wearier than when I'd arrived. My train announced itself with a rush of cold air and I boarded, claimed a row to myself, and exhaled, collapsing against the vinyl seat, relieved to be in my own company once again. The moments alone, I had realized awhile back, were so rarely the lonely ones.

***

It was the technician I saw most regularly who called me back for blood work, giving me a big smile when our eyes met. "Hi! I said excitedly, "how are you?" adding, before she could even reply, "I'm back!" That part was obvious, though I couldn't help but say it out loud. After an ectopic pregnancy, two surgeries, and three sluggish months of waiting, I was showing up at the clinic to begin a long-awaited fifth IVF cycle. It was the promise of a baby that had me giddy, the hope that came with starting again. Coming face to face with the technician, as well as my doctor and nurses, was a homecoming of sorts. If I belonged anywhere, it was here.

"Welcome back!" The technician replied. "It's so good to see you." I pushed the sleeve of my shirt high enough so it bunched above my elbow. "It's been so strange not coming in, how have you been? Has it been busy?" We chatted with ease and buoyancy as she drew my blood, my veins plump and fresh after so much time off. Afterward, she led me to an exam room where muscle memory kicked in; I disrobed from the waist down, shrouded my bare legs with a brittle paper covering, and waited for the doctor. I lay back for a bit, then sat up, fidgeting with my hands as I waited for the knock. "Come in!" My doctor and the technician entered and the mere sight of his white coat perked me up even more. "I'm *BACK*!" This time I emphasized the words with two arms thrust into the air.

"Welcome back," he replied dryly. I bristled through my bubbles at the obvious disparity between his greeting and mine, but I continued smiling at him expectantly. As he walked over to the sink he started talking, and not about my triumphant return. "I just

159

diagnosed an ectopic in the other room," he continued, noticeably preoccupied. "I never see ectopics. What did you do, bring some kind of ectopic juju in here today?"

There was something peer-like to the dynamic between my doctor and me. We were the same age, for one thing, and I would often remark to Tim how odd it was to think we could have drunk beers with him in high school. I became a patient only four months into his practice, which, I imagine, was a significant time for him. He oversaw my care in the cycle that led to my ectopic, was the person to cut me open to remove it, then saw me through a second surprise surgery after that. We knew each other in what felt like a meaningful way, leading to a familiar, casual quality in our doctor-patient relationship, which, I suppose, is what led to this moment.

My smile went dark, my fizz ran flat. From a man in a white lab coat, whose judgment I held in the highest regard, and under whose supervision I felt safe and cared for, these words rang out not as a flippant joke but as a sort of pronouncement both medical and supernatural; I was cursed. Here I had bounded into the office, positively giddy to be reunited with my people, only to contaminate the place with my toxic energy. "Oh my God, really?" I said softly, the horror of it dawning on me. "That's terrible." There was a look of regret on my doctor's face almost immediately; he knew he shouldn't have said it. "Yep, she's going up to the hospital now. Anyway, let's take a look and see what's going on with you. How've you been?"

While it's not accurate to say I loved spending time at the fertility clinic, I did love having a place to go, where everyone was singularly invested in the same thing; where we all spoke offhandedly of ICSI and blasts and gonadotropins; where everything I was dealing with was considered completely normal; where I splayed my bare bottom on the white paper sheet covering the exam table, my pants and underwear in a heap nearby, with less hesitation than I agreed to meet close friends for dinner. Over the months and years of infertility my world had gotten smaller, until this place was pretty much all I had. To be unwelcome here was to be thoroughly, unimaginably alone.

My doctor performed the exam, said some stuff I didn't entirely follow about a cyst and a corpus luteum, and without thinking about it, my responses matched his in brevity and clinical tone. When I dressed and walked out, it was with the gait of an entirely different person than the one who'd entered. I sat slumped on the subway home, scanning defaced ads above me and the faces of strangers across the way before lowering my head and directing my gaze toward my lap. My hands were resting there, knotted into themselves, a tense bundle of knuckles and nails, holding tight to each other.

# Defiance

When a dark, bubbling geyser erupted from the vein of my outstretched arm, blood of remarkable reach and velocity, I had a feeling it was going to be a bad night.

It was a routine IV injection, after all; there was no reason for me to be bleeding. I had just changed into my hospital gown and was settling into my ER room when Maggie, the nurse assigned to me that night, came in to insert the needle and get me all hooked up. The veins of my left arm—blue and bulbous, with a serpentine elegance—are preferable to those of my right; it was one of the few certainties about my body I had to show for all these years of treatment.

I can't remember if I shared that with Maggie, helped steer her toward the better vein, but it was indeed my left side she was hovering over, holding the butterfly needle at a low angle near the crook of my arm, sliding the silver point into one solitary vessel. It should have been textbook. So why did the blood start spurting until the white hospital sheets were in grisly disarray? Maggie looked young—25 maybe—but something told me it wasn't inexperience that had caused the botched insertion. It was a little hint—a warning—that on this night, I was in for a bloody fucking mess.

***

The better part of a month had passed since the surgery to remove my ectopic pregnancy, and I had gone into the clinic for blood work to find out where I was in my cycle. Hours later, my doctor called, with something unexpected to share. "I was very surprised to see there is still hCG in your system," I heard him explain.

It didn't make sense. My hCG—the pregnancy hormone—should have been zero. They'd removed the pregnancy *and* my fallopian tube, to guard against this very thing. "It's gone down significantly," he said, "but some hCG is lingering." I don't remember his explanation for why what should have been an open-and-shut transition from pregnant to not had morphed into a drawn-out ordeal—a slow burn, the death of a star. I do know that it did not strike me as dangerous but more of a nuisance. I had hoped my period would be arriving any day now, allowing us to get on with treatment.

It took only a couple of days for things to get stranger. My doctor measured the hCG in my blood again a few days later and, most unexpectedly, it had gone up. The pregnancy hormone was getting stronger, not weaker. But how could that be? We had only transferred one embryo, so it wasn't possible that another pregnancy had taken hold. My doctor was confounded—and concerned. He explained that a clump of pregnancy cells had seemingly been left behind, likely attaching itself somewhere in the vicinity of my reproductive organs. And because pregnancy cells are rapidly growing, this little cluster was clinging to my body, determinedly duplicating itself again and again.

I had been standing at the stove with my phone in one hand, pushing clusters of meat through hissing oil with the other, as I listened to this latest update. We had become accustomed to bad news, but this—the absurdity of it, the profound cruelty—felt different. I wasn't pregnant. I had lost my tube. And yet I was being held prisoner by a sprinkling of dust that somehow remained. Haunted by the shadow of the baby I would never have. We were no longer free to mourn his absence. It was as if, unbeknownst to us, the lost pregnancy and severed body part that had housed it had been the easy part. Now we were contending with the surreal understanding that the absent, in fact, had a presence, that my body had become the physical embodiment of negative space.

The existence of these rogue cells wasn't the only concern; the question of their location was critical and would determine how this would all be resolved. If they had attached to the lining of my uterus, for example, they would be flushed out naturally when I got my period. If they had affixed themselves elsewhere, they would keep replicating, stubbornly holding my body hostage until I was given a drug powerful enough to kill them. That drug would stay in my system for three months, so it would also kill our chances of trying again for that duration, the equivalent of eternity.

I thrust the wooden spoon at Tim and escaped the kitchen, the scorch and sizzle of turkey chili suddenly overloading my senses. "I don't understand," was all I could say. "How is this even possible? When will we find out where the cells are?" I could hear empathy in his voice as he informed me that the answer could not be fast-tracked. There was no way of knowing until I got my period, and we measured the hCG again. At that point it would either be present or absent; that's how we would know. "I'm really sorry, Amy."

I had spent the previous three-plus weeks tending to my physical scars: keeping them hidden behind gauze in the shower, gliding a fingertip full of arnica along the incisions once they had knit together enough for me to touch them. Slowly I returned to exercise, easing into myself again, recalibrating after the shock of trauma. To learn all that healing had been pointless, that I had not moved forward even an inch into the future but was unknowingly trapped inside the day of my surgery, that the entire nightmare of that cycle wasn't over, that, according to my hCG at least, I was still a little bit pregnant—it was quite literally beyond my imagining. When I hung up the phone I turned to Tim and spewed the news in a fit of tears and hysteria.

That was Monday. By Thursday night we sat across from each other at the kitchen counter, the pendant lights above us glowing, finishing the last of the Italian beef sandwiches Tim's sister had shipped us as a very kind get-well gesture after my surgery. After retreating to the couch, it wasn't long before I started to sense the food wasn't sitting right. That's all it was, a little indigestion. But then I made the slightest movement, rearranging myself against the cushions, and I felt it: a pain I can only describe as wrong. A pain without category. A pain that didn't exist on a scale of 1-10 but in some other realm, classified by some other numerical system in which I was not fluent. A pain that was Other. It was immediately followed by a deep, involuntary inhale, because I had known that pain from a few weeks earlier.

"I'm going to bed," I told Tim abruptly as I rose from the couch. I would do my best to deny this, I would go to sleep. I sat on the toilet, hopeful it was indigestion, or maybe even my period. But I knew. I switched off the light, climbed into bed, and lay there, knowing. Trying to will the knowledge away while my consciousness took the time it needed to reckon with the truth. To acknowledge the depth of this dense, round abdominal pain that was bubbling up at 10 p.m., just as I wanted to go to sleep. I flicked the light back on and walked into the living room to tell Tim. He hovered over me as I dialed my clinic's answering service and left a message, getting a call back minutes later. "Based on your symptoms, and what we know about the residual pregnancy cells, I think you need to come in right now." Wonderful.

When Tim and I walked into the Emergency Room together, I felt an odd confidence, a little bit like a pro. I had been there so recently, I half expected to have the chance to introduce him to my friend nurse Caroline. But it was Maggie who showed me to my room this time, who gave me the gown to change into, who said she'd be right back to check my vitals. Maggie was a bit younger, and not quite as effortless as Caroline, but she, too, soon felt like a friend.

Maggie looked sheepish after the botched IV incident. "I'm so sorry," she said. "Let's try this again." After she asked if I wouldn't mind getting off the bed so she could remove and replace the linens, her second attempt went perfectly.

It was probably midnight by the time I was hooked up, on clean sheets, being offered morphine for my pain. "I'm ok," I told them. "I don't need it." Which was true. The sensation in my lower abdomen was tolerable. But it is also true that my instinct is always to tough it out. No Tylenol for a headache, no narcotics after surgery, no morphine now. Looking back, I'm pretty sure that refusing the drugs was also my way of refusing to acknowledge what was happening. I hadn't been offered morphine at my last ER visit, and I didn't like that it was being suggested now.

Beneath the dim hospital lighting, I in my bed, Tim in a chair pushed up against the wall, we waited for an ultrasound, busying ourselves with our phones as the collision between the life I had so recently been living and my present reality settled in. I was signed up for an exercise class the next morning, and it was past the cutoff for their cancellation policy so I would be charged for the class no matter what. Fuck. Maybe I could send an email and explain the situation. I thought about how tomorrow was Friday, and how thank God it wasn't last Friday, because that had been my due date for a freelance writing assignment. The close call of a potentially missed deadline had me muttering mentally; *see, this is why I shouldn't be taking on any projects at all, because this is all such a fucking disaster and who can commit to anything in the midst of this fucking process where everything is so uncertain and fucked up and clearly anything that can go wrong will go fucking wrong. Just, fuck!*

The progression of irritability corresponded directly to the progression of pain. The sensation in my belly was becoming a hollow drumbeat, growing more insistent, more thrumming, harder to ignore; I was ready for the morphine. Tim popped out of the room to flag someone down, and I bit down on my lip as I asked if I could maybe just start slow. *The pain is getting worse, but I only want a little.*

Maggie understood. She administered a low dose of morphine and stayed for a bit as the thrum dulled. "Don't worry," she told me, "I think we'll probably wind up giving you the methotrexate, and that will resolve it. You're going to walk out of here just fine." She meant to reassure me, but methotrexate was the drug that would stay in my system for three months. I got teary. "I already had surgery to remove this pregnancy, I just don't understand why this is happening, it's been a really long road, and not being able to do another cycle for three months, I can't even explain it, like I'm sure that sounds like nothing but it's just a really big deal for us." She spoke softly. "I know. I've been reading through your chart."

It should have been obvious; of course she would look through my records. She was doing her job. But still, I was moved to know she actually cared. When were she, Caroline, and I all going out for margs?

The minutes ticked, the pain roiled, the morphine dripped. A stream of familiar faces—Maggie, a resident, an OB/GYN, the reproductive endocrinologist overseeing things—cycled through my room, checking pain levels while I waited to be seen by a radiologist. At one point, presumably when one of my main caretakers had gone on break, a face I didn't recognize appeared, a tall woman with dark hair and dark blue scrubs, to very casually administer my morphine, as though she too had been doing it for hours. This nurse lacked Maggie's gentle touch as well as, it seemed, her interest in my chart, because within minutes of her visit my anatomy registered a much more powerful dose of the opiate. My cheeks and forehead turned cold and wet, my stomach bottomed out into my feet and a hurricane swirl of nausea rose up in its place. "I feel sick," I said, impulse moving me toward the side of the bed to try to stand, "I'm going to be sick." Tim thrust his head into the hallway, "can someone help, she's going to throw up!" I couldn't stand so instead I sat hunched forward, heaving over the foot of my bed, head slick, heart hammering, and a resident rushed to place a plastic vomit container in front of me.

We had learned precisely how much morphine my body could handle. Another nurse added an anti-nausea to my cocktail drip.

Around 2 a.m. I was wheeled in to see the radiologist. I had only ever been ultra-sounded in small check-up rooms, and what stood out to me was how cavernous this space was by contrast. I recall two distinct areas, separated by loads of equipment, and in my memory (which, to be fair, was distorted by pain and drugs), there was another patient being evaluated at the same time. Was that standard protocol for Emergency Room radiology? I had no idea.

What *is* still vivid to me is writhing around on that examining table. The man administering the ultrasound inserted the vaginal wand and set off on his exploration, probing, twisting, jabbing the device inside of me to record image after image, angle after angle of my reproductive system, each new prod searing through me. My body involuntarily contorted itself each time to lessen the sensation, like a fish flopping on a dock trying to wriggle her way off the hook. It went on and on and on. Finally, the man broke the silence; "You're almost done." Almost, but not quite. So it continued, what felt like being stabbed with a dull blade from the inside out.

I was shaken by the pain. This was scary pain. Pain powerful enough to pierce through hours of a morphine drip. Back in my ER room I closed my eyes and lay still.

The doctor most closely observing me that night, the one I'd first shared my symptoms with over the phone, sat down with us around 4 a.m. He was not yet a member of the fertility clinic's practice, he was still in the process of completing his fellowship, and his face told the story of a doctor who'd been on his feet in a hospital for at least 24 hours. I can picture him taking off his glasses and rubbing his eyes. We stared at him expectantly. A mash of words came out. *Left ovary. Bleeding. Unknown cause.* He started drawing a diagram on a piece of paper. *Source unclear. Have to find out.* It was tough to make sense of what he was trying to tell us but after a bit of talking I hardened; I had heard enough. Tim was still not following. "Sorry," he said. "I don't understand, can you explain what this means?" "They're going back in," I snapped, my hands resting on my distended belly, firmly full of blood. "I'm having another surgery." "Wait, what?" Tim was disbelieving. He was also angry. "You don't know what's wrong but you're going to open her up again? I honestly don't understand."

The ultrasound pictures had revealed some sort of irregularity on my left ovary, with blood leaking into my abdomen, though the actual source of the issue remained undetermined. The only way to find out would be to open up those still-fresh scars, pull back my same tired skin, so they could get their eyes on it. "I understand it's disconcerting that we can't tell you what exactly is happening," the doctor offered, "but we're going to figure it out and get it taken care of." At the outset of the entire baffling mess that was trying for a baby, I had imagined I could grasp onto facts, pick up on clues, reason my way through this thing. I would work harder than I'd ever worked in my life to seize control, to make this happen. And if controlling the process of getting pregnant wasn't possible, then I would settle for understanding what was (or, let's face it, wasn't) happening, and why. Never did I consider that this mystery might prove unsolvable. That surrendering to a never-ending series of unknowns might be my only option.

The doctor produced the paperwork I would have to sign to authorize what was about to happen, and it was jarringly open-ended. Not knowing what they would find, they needed preemptive permission to do just about anything. Would I allow them to remove blood, ovaries, my one remaining fallopian tube, whatever it took? I looked at Tim and signed my name. There was no real choice.

I have no idea what we did or said once we were alone in the room again. I'm sure we talked, spit out words about how fucked up this was, how insane that this was happening again. Or maybe we sat in silence, our lonely minds whirring, too caught up in our own anxieties to extend each other any real comfort. Maggie came in, she had heard the plan, she wanted to check on me. Throughout the night we had agreed we wouldn't tell our families what was going on until we knew more. It was the very early morning and a phone ringing in any of our parents' houses at that hour would cause unnecessary worry, so we decided that Tim would reach out to everyone once I was actually in surgery. It seemed crazy no one knew we were here, but there wasn't anything they could have done anyway.

Around 5 a.m. one of my regular fertility doctor's colleagues, a man I'd never met before, walked into my room. Upbeat and calming, he told me that he would be my surgeon; he had just driven in from his home in Connecticut and they pushed his schedule for the day so I could be done first. He peeked at my incisions and remarked cheerfully about what a good job my last surgeon had done. He seemed thoroughly undaunted by all of it, and I felt my first glimmer of reassurance. The doctor explained they'd be going back in through those same slits, and while they couldn't tell the exact issue from the imaging, as soon as they opened me up they should have a better picture, and they would get me in and out as fast as possible. After he walked out, I overheard him calling my doctor. "Hey there, so I have Amy Ryan here, she's had some complications, we're going to take a look and find out what's going on. Uh huh. Yep. Yep." I tried to imagine the other side of that call—had my doctor been jolted out of sleep by his phone? Or had he answered from his car, already driving into work to begin monitoring patients for the day? He knew every agonizing detail of what had gone on throughout this cycle; what on earth did he make of this?

Maggie gave me a little smile from behind her desk, waving goodbye as I was wheeled on a gurney to the OR. Her belief that I'd be given a pill and sent home seemed so quaint now; surely we'd laugh about it over drinks. We deposited Tim in the waiting room, he gave me a kiss and told me he loved me. We locked eyes, his arms bracing the metal perimeter of the bed; it's going to be ok. "She should be out in about 45 minutes," the doctor told him. "I'll come and find you as soon as we're done."

The surgery, I learned later, wound up taking twice that long, so Tim had a nice chunk of time to sip burnt hospital coffee and pace the room. He called my sister first, around 7:30 a.m., setting in motion a familial chain of panic.

I've tried to picture myself on the operating room table in that hour and a half where memory doesn't exist; eyes closed, mouth obscured by a breathing tube, hospital gown pulled up to show skin and parts, my scars, still fresh enough to be a jarringly different shade than the flesh surrounding them, sliced through once more. Wounds trying their hardest to heal, ripped back open. I can see that person, yet I do not feel as though I am that person.

***

Here are the uncontested facts. The scientific truth of what happened, per my medical records:

**After suitable GETA, the patient was prepped and draped in sterile fashion, and placed in dorsal lithotomy position. A weighted speculum was placed in the vagina, and a single-tooth tenaculum to grasp the cervix. The cervix was dilated to accommodate a small curette, and a gentle curettage was performed, and this tissue was sent off to Pathology for evaluation. At the completion of this, a**

Foley catheter had been placed into the bladder before, and a HUMI catheter was then placed into the uterus. A 5 mm infraumbilical incision was made in the area of the previous incision, and the abdomen was then insufflated with CO2 to a maximum pressure of 15 mmHg with a Veress needle. Once completed, the 5 mm Visiport trocar was placed through this incision, and the above-mentioned findings were noted. A right and left Visiport were then placed under direct visualization. At this point, the pelvis and abdomen were suctioned of blood. The above-mentioned findings were noted. The right tube was status post salpingectomy. The left tube was normal. The left ovary had a moderately sized cyst that was actively bleeding from the cyst itself. This appeared that maybe this was an ectopic ovarian pregnancy tissue in the left ovary. This was incised with monopolar cautery, and the cyst wall was opened. The tissue was removed, and what appeared to be a cyst or corpus luteum cyst was removed from this area also. Once this was removed, the inside of the cyst wall now appeared smooth. This was cauterized with bipolar cautery for hemostasis. This was controlled, and as irrigated and aspirated, and hemostasis was found to be excellent. There were no other areas of ectopic pregnancy tissue or bleeding from any other areas in the pelvis or visualized abdominal contents. The liver was visualized, the omentum was visualized, the sigmoid and rectum were visualized, and these were found to be normal without pathology. All clots were then removed from the cavity. The patient's upper abdomen was then inspected and found to have a significant amount of blood up by the liver, and this was aspirated. The patient was then placed in reverse Trendelenburg to aspirate this as much as we could, out of the pelvis. At this point hemostasis was excellent. The gas was desufflated, hemostasis was assured with the low-pressure system, and the gas was then desufflated fully. The trocars were removed. The incisions were closed with 4-0 Biosyn in subcuticular fashion, after all of the gas had been sufflated. The incisions were closed with 4-0 Biosyn in subcuticular fashion. Steri-Strips were applied. Bandages were applied, and 0.25% Marcaine was injected into each of the incisions.

The light was golden, warm, inviting, much softer than typical February sunshine, with dust particles dancing through. Tim, seated in a chair next to my bed, perked up when he saw my eyes flutter open. "Hi," he said gently, leaning toward me. "It went great, you did great." I wasn't aware of any pain—any sensation at all, really. My eyelids were heavy, and I was so, so tired, but the absence of pain and the glory of sunlight felt transformative. Through the fog I was clear about the one question I needed answered: "Did they take anything out? Do I still have my ovaries?" Tim's response was immediate. "They didn't take anything. Everything is good. Try to close your eyes and get some more rest." He turned out to be right— my organs were all intact—but I eventually learned that when he said this, he had no idea if it was true. He hadn't thought to ask the doctor directly. But this reassurance, expressed with authority, spilled right off his tongue because it was the only answer he was willing to give. I nodded, satisfied, closed my eyes, and drifted away again.

I was in and out of consciousness for all my hours in that little space, what I later learned to be Recovery One. A celestial ether cocooned me as the world spun all around, my awareness coming in intermittent spurts. Through closed eyes, I heard Tim on the phone talking to our families. Later, a nurse appeared to draw blood. When I looked on my phone, there was an email from a friend who was just checking in—did she somehow know I was here? Then, suddenly, my sister's voice broke through. She was right there, standing next to me, having driven into Manhattan from the suburbs to see how I was doing. I experienced that day as a series of moments separated by indeterminate amounts of time. It was like a dream sequence in a movie musical: all poetry, no plot.

My alertness peaked when the fellow who'd been overseeing my care pulled back the curtain of my little stall. I joked about the fact that he was still on call after all this time. "My shift is ending now," he smiled, looking far more relaxed than he had the previous night. He asked how I was feeling, and then started telling us about my surgery.

"You lost a liter of blood," the doctor shared after asking how I was doing. "It was a *lot*." He went on to explain how they'd discovered the clump of pregnancy cells had attached to a cyst on my left ovary. As the cells multiplied, the cyst had burst, and caused a significant amount of internal bleeding. "It was up to here," he said emphatically, holding his hand up to the middle of his breastbone. "Medically," he smiled sheepishly, "it was awesome." I laughed, because he said it with a look that acknowledged it had been decidedly less awesome for me. I imagined a suction inhaling clumps of blood and mystery matter, my organs bobbing in a sea of red, and felt a strange pride, through my haze, of that awesomeness. There was other news, things still being biopsied, confusion over whether, irrespective of the cyst, there had been something else involving ectopic cells on my left ovary. It remains a mystery to this day, at least according to my medical records, where the findings of my surgery include an actual question mark.

**Findings: 1,000 cc hemoperitoneum with clots. Left ovarian cyst with bleeding and ? pregnancy tissue. No evidence of ectopic tissue on omentum or bowel or in CDS. Right ovary normal. Left ovary normal.**

Someone held up a phone—it might have been the fellow, it might have been Tim—and suddenly my doctor's voice was in my ear. "It's been quite a night," I told him. "So I've heard. How are you feeling?" He shared that due to the significant loss of blood I'd experienced, they were keeping me in this initial Recovery area until some tests came back, which would determine whether I would need a blood transfusion. *If you do need additional blood, I just want to tell you that the odds of getting HIV are very low—they're about such and such in such and such.* This was meant to be reassuring; in truth, it was horrifying. His words punctured my golden bubble. What was even happening right now? How in God's name did I get here? How in the hell was I listening to someone tell me my odds of contracting HIV? I was just trying to have a baby.

In the end there was no transfusion needed. My HIV odds that day returned to a much more comfortable zero. Eventually I was moved from Recovery One to Recovery Two, where it took several hours and more than one episode of vomiting to be able to stand up, walk across the room, and empty my bladder—otherwise known as the "Pee Test"—which was the criteria that needed to be met for me to go home.

\*\*\*

In the days afterward, a series of linear bruises wrapped themselves around one side of my waist. They resembled the striations within a tree, the concentric circles at its core hidden beneath the bark that tell all the secrets of that wood's life. My rings had risen to the surface, though, my secrets exposed for all to see. The bruising descended down to my labia, which was a disturbing shade of purple, puffed up and firm to the touch. My doctor assured me it was from all the blood that had been in my belly. "What about the spasm in my leg I felt earlier?" I asked. "Could it be a blood clot?" I called the answering service one night, reporting tingling throughout my arm and excessive beating in my heart. I was told the blood loss had left me anemic; I should eat steak and spinach and take an iron supplement. There was nothing prescribed for the terror I felt regarding what unimaginable surprise my body had in store next.

\*\*\*

Years later I was in the hospital waiting room, which was packed yet soundless, when I felt someone's eyes on me, walking over. "Do you remember me?" he asked, sitting down in the chair beside mine. It was the fellow who'd been on call that night. Of course I remembered. "I saw your name on the schedule and wanted to come say hello. I remember your surgery very well. How are you doing?" This man who had seen my blood up to there; who had witnessed this bizarre, unlikely complication from an (uncommon in itself) ectopic pregnancy; this freak surgery I still don't know how to explain on medical history forms. It had stayed with him. He knew my name. I missed the part he recalled best—the slicing and suctioning, the cystic tissue and unexplained cells and abundance of blood. But the rest of that night, every bit of it, belongs to me.

# Envy

***

You might think that hearing a friend announce, "I'm pregnant!" would be the worst possible thing. Oh, but it isn't. What's worse is hearing that friend who has not yet shared her news say something far more innocuous: "Can I just get a seltzer?"

It's a harmless-sounding request, but the drink sets in motion a chemical reaction, dissolving the congenial atmosphere, bloating the air with bubbles, an entire unsuspecting dinner table done in by carbonation. I can't count how many pregnancies I learned of this way, how many meals I spent in obsessive anticipation: *Will she announce it at this very table, this very night?* I'd clutch the stem of my wine glass, keeping it close to my lips for support, the lapse of time between deducing the news and actually being told spent in a sort of white-knuckle state. *Will she tell us in a group or do it one-on-one? Will she hold out until 12 weeks or share earlier?* If I could prepare myself, see it coming, arrange my face properly, then maybe, just maybe, it wouldn't hurt quite so badly.

Cristina's tell was ginger ale, not seltzer, but as soon as she requested it, I looked up from my menu. Cristina had never not drank alcohol at dinner. *Oh God*, I leaned back in my chair. *Not her too.* Cristina and Alex had gotten married *two* years after Tim and me. The day I stood up as her matron of honor, I already had 12 frustrating months of trying under my belt.

I envied every one of my friends who got pregnant, the fact of it as well as the ease with which it happened. That they got to conceive their children normally, working with the natural order of

177

the universe instead of against it. Sex with their husbands, the old "he just looks at me and I get pregnant!" (which, please, fertile people—stop saying). Envious that their babies were spontaneously made instead of forced into being. That their children were made of love and skin and sweat and sunshine, and mine, if ever they were to be, would be made of science. Does that even matter? I often questioned. Does the energy and method of how a baby is made seep into their little soul? I envied all the people that didn't have to wonder.

I was particularly upset by all the pregnancies that defied my internalized set of rules about how motherhood was supposed to unfold. Namely, that she who got married first should get pregnant first. It was a fundamental belief embedded deep in my psyche, one I wasn't even aware of until I found myself protesting again and again, *She got married way after me, how on earth is she pregnant already?* I liked the idea of order and process, that if we all took our place in line, my turn to conspicuously order seltzer would come before long. And holy hell, was that drink going to taste good.

It was a year after Cristina's wedding, one summer weekend at her parents' house in Rhode Island, when she revealed that they, too, had started to try. Since the day Cristina and I met moving into our freshman dorm at college, our lives have braided together again and again. First as English majors and suitemates, then when we both moved to New York City after graduation, attending a summer publishing course, making our way into the magazine industry, and, eventually, as colleagues at the same magazine, working side-by-side for several years.

Sometimes I found it comforting to have so many stages of my life and career overlap with hers; other times it made me claustrophobic. We saw the same hairdresser for our equally impossibly curly hair, hers brunette, mine blonde, and had the same astrological sign. We shared the same old friends from college and the same new ones from magazines. Collectively, it amounted to an odd sort of synergy, albeit one that threatened to jeopardize my own sense of self. Sometimes, I wanted to occupy my own distinct space on this earth, to feel like my path and my choices were unlike anybody else's. Besides, having Cristina right there, a perpetual presence, made for a continual point of comparison; when I held myself up to her as my mirror, my inadequacies often stared right back.

Waiting outside on a table for brunch near the beach that overcast morning in Rhode Island, we leaned against the sea wall, waves slamming on rocks below, everything grey. I can't remember exactly how Cristina broke the news that they were now going for a baby. All I recall is my own sense of doom. *Please no. Please no. Please no.* By then, Tim and I had been spinning our wheels for two full years. She seemed hesitant to speak, shrugging her shoulders and acknowledging that of course none of us could know how long it would take. But I'd seen enough friends fly past me on this journey; I understood exactly where we were headed, and who would be getting there first.

Sure enough, she was ordering ginger ale within a matter of months. Despite the obvious implications, and the fact that I died a little inside, we both ignored her drink choice, mutually agreeing to pretend it was normal, and instead spent our time catching up on her trip to California and my recent miscarriage (one topic decidedly more upbeat than the other!). All the while, my inner self embarked on its own unfiltered diatribe, nearly drowning out our conversation, her words thick and muted to my ears, as if we were talking under water. *Holy fuck, I cannot believe this is happening. I knew it. Of course she got pregnant that easily. That was, like, what, two months?? I fucking knew this was going to happen but also, how the fuck is this happening?* Cristina, presumably nauseous, picked over much of her dinner, and I was quick to turn down dessert. I was ready to go. When we hugged each other goodbye beneath the awning out front, it was as if we were teenagers at the sock hop kept at arms-length by an inflated balloon. Except what distanced us was invisible, an obstruction the approximate size of a full-term pregnant belly.

With the events of that evening, a new phase began in my relationship with Cristina, a complicated dance that shifted between revealing and withholding, between *just tell me already*, and *please, whatever you do, don't say it out loud*. Cristina was the lead in our two-woman performance. She would be the one to decide when to share, how to make it known, while I was dragged around the floor, flung this way and that, doing everything I could to keep my feet beneath me. I already felt so powerless within my own body, inside my own life, Cristina's announcement just one more thing that would be thrust upon me without warning, like a surprise and unwelcome dip.

We danced this way for an entire month. The night Tim and I went over for dinner, Cristina texted to say she wasn't planning on drinking, but wondered if she should get a bottle of wine for us. *Of course I'm fucking drinking*, I thought bitterly; under normal circumstances that would have gone without saying. But I responded cheerfully. *Yes! Probably. If you guys aren't though, don't worry about it, we'll pick stuff up.* She was wearing an oversized t-shirt and chunky cardigan when she opened the door a few hours later, and as I tried to steal secret glances at her tummy, I felt certain that this would be the night. Instead, I swallowed chunks of pork and potatoes and made conversation, awaiting an announcement that never came. *Maybe she was waiting for me?* I wondered, but there was no way I would push her to reveal before she was ready.

More weeks passed and we engaged in our normal emails and texts about holiday plans and television shows, work assignments and future outings, with no mention of a baby. We sashayed around the thing that mattered, neither one of us daring to touch it.

I arrived at our lunch first, opting to wait at the table instead of languishing by the hostess stand. Cristina showed up a few minutes later with an effusive hello and a flurry of tote bags and cold-weather gear, which she dismantled before collapsing into the seat across from mine. I was feeling particularly upbeat that Friday, our fourth IVF cycle was newly underway, my period arriving just in time to start up with our new doctor before the end of the year, and the current of optimism charging through me was stronger than it had been in months. "Hi," I said excitedly, "this is so fun! I never have lunch with anyone anymore." Cristina flashed all her teeth. "I know! It's such a treat."

We skimmed over our menus and exchanged top-line updates, eventually settling into a rhythm of conversation. It was then that Cristina asked how this new cycle was going. "I *love* our new doctor," I began emphatically. "I feel really confident with him, switching was absolutely the right call. He texts and calls and is the one I see in the morning for monitoring, so he's really hands on and couldn't be more different than the last guy, and I truly trust that he's going to be able to help us." Cristina was nodding happily. "That's so great, Amy. And you knew it, you totally trusted your gut. And look, it's already paying off."

I remember expressing my good news, and the next thing I recall is her sharing *her* good news, though there must have been a segue in there somewhere; we couldn't have jumped right from my IVF to her pregnancy. Maybe it was when I eventually dared to ask something open-ended, an innocuous, "what's happening with you?" I don't know whether it was because she was a few weeks further along, or that my clear-eyed enthusiasm about our new cycle made me appear happy and well enough to receive the information, but Cristina decided to go for it. "Welllllll," she drew out the word, staring down at her plate as she paused long enough for me to understand what was about to happen. "I'm pregnant!!!!" She was beaming. I gasped a little, heat rising to my cheeks.

"Oh my God, Cristina! That is so exciting! When are you due?" Quickly the details began to tumble, and as I listened, I felt myself unclench; the anticipation was over, though what replaced it wasn't much better. Hearing her excitement in sharing her due date, how sick she'd been feeling, that she'd know the gender in a week or so—I found it hard to stay in my seat. To endure the knowledge that she had been handed everything I wanted—and so quickly. I have no idea what my face looked like, but I did my best to smile, nod, ask questions, muster up every bit of what I was capable of giving as a friend.

Outside the restaurant, we said goodbye beneath snowflakes that had just started meandering to the ground. "Thank you for telling me," I said, trying to convey the truth and weight of my words through the pressure of our embrace. "Oh my God, of course!" she replied. "Thank you for being excited for me." We parted ways, walking in opposite directions down the sidewalk, freezing tears slipping down my cheeks. The dance was over.

***

The red onesie I clutched walking into the hospital to meet Jessie's baby was something of a security blanket—for me, that is, not for the baby. It was an Etsy find, the Notorious B.I.G. lyrics, *Spread love it's the Brooklyn way*, scrawled across the front. After my ho-hum registry present at her shower, this felt personal and thoughtful, something I was excited to give. We'd sung that line at least a million times in high school—driving around in Jessie's car, packed shoulder-to-shoulder at house parties—and now that I found myself a Brooklyn resident two decades later, it felt poetic to gift something that so artfully tied our past and present. Plus, the sentiment spoke to me, and I hoped it would communicate something about the spirit in which I was there. That despite starting up our fifth round of IVF, and how very desperately I wanted a baby of my own, that I wasn't here harboring bitterness or jealousy. I was here in love.

I envied the idea of my friends' babies. I envied the blossoming tummies in which they grew and the admission they granted into the club of motherhood. But I was discovering that once those pregnancies were over and there was an actual, physical human in the world, it felt different, not quite as painful. It was impossible not to be moved and overcome by all that is profound and touching about new life. I found my soul stirred by these innocent, perfect little people springing forth from my closest friends.

When I entered the hospital room, a lactation consultant was hovering over Jessie, trying to help her get Benjamin to latch. The sash of her robe was untied, exposing her tummy and breasts in a post-partum puddle, her wrinkly baby, just 36 hours old, pressed up against her flesh. The consultant was guiding Jessie's hold, arranging Benjamin, a picture of tangled limbs so raw and intimate I felt a heightened sense of not belonging and hurried to tuck myself into a corner of the room.

When the woman left, Jessie re-tied her robe and gave me a tired smile. "Hi!" my mouth was wide as I offered an excited wave of my hand, crossing the room to hand her flowers. My eyes were already misting. "You did it!" I hugged her, trying to be gentle. "I can't believe he's here. And oh my God, Jessie, it's a boy!!!" While we talked, Benjamin slept nearby in his clear hospital bed, a glorified plastic box lined with blankets, and I glanced back and forth between him and my sleepy, elated friend, who looked as much like herself as she did entirely changed. She told me all about labor, the details of how he finally arrived, their plans for leaving the hospital the following day.

"I won't stay long," I promised, "I know you all are still just getting to know each other." "No, it's fine!" Jessie protested. "Do you want to hold him?" "Yes," I said. "I would love to." Jessie's husband, Chris, reached in to pick him up and place him in my arms, and I smiled down at the perfect slope of his pink head, took in his miniscule features that already looked so much like my friend's, the shape of his eyes, the arch of his nose, and felt the solid, warm weight of him. A bundle of air with such impossible gravity. When it was time for Benjamin to eat again, I passed him back and made my way toward the door. "Thank you so much for coming," Jessie said, as we exchanged one last hug. "Of course! This was so special, I can't believe I got to meet him on his second day on earth. I will never forget it."

I emerged from the hospital into cold sunshine, stuffing my hands into my coat pockets as I hurried past weeks-old snow. I was headed uptown, to see *Going Clear*, a documentary on Scientology, of all things, which was playing near Lincoln Center. I figured I'd make the most of my trip into Manhattan. By the time I crept into the theater, the previews and opening credits had finished, so it was a hurried entry into the world of religious power and devotion, indoctrination and manipulation. It was a jolt, from warm newborn cradled in my arms to cold, anonymous theater, empty seats on either side of me, darkness magnified up front. But it provided a welcome sort of intermediate space. I couldn't have held Benjamin and gone straight back to my empty apartment.

Instead, I lost myself amidst the other people there that day, who, for all I know, were taking note of *me*. Observing my unencumbered self, tethered to no one, so entirely without responsibilities as to be able to see a movie midday, no coin-sized mouth searching for my nipple, no sweaty palm reaching for mine, no school pick-up interrupting my leisure. For all I know, in that nearly empty movie theater in the middle of a Thursday afternoon, I was the picture of everything someone most coveted: a still-young woman able to savor solitude, silence, freedom. Envy is funny that way.

# *Hope*

***

If my Hope existed in the physical world it would look like a long-sleeved 3-6 month onesie I picked up for $4.99 on clearance at Gap.

We had been trying for less than a year when I bought the onesie for the soon-to-be-born daughter of a childhood friend, tossing it in my cart because it was sweet and cost five dollars. The lavender stars and round fish were adorably innocent but not too cutesy, and I liked that it was intended for a girl but a boy could probably get away with wearing it, too. But then I found other treasures to give the little girl I was shopping for that day, so I kept the onesie, knowing another friend would welcome another baby soon enough.

Only when they did, I wouldn't relinquish the onesie. I can't remember how many times I pulled that onesie out of the shopping bag, held it at arm's length, then returned it to the back of my closet. At first it was because picking out new baby gifts was more fun than giving one I already had, but as time passed, I started making excuses for keeping it. And somewhere along the way, I realized that this particular onesie couldn't be a gift. It belonged to our baby.

There was not one remarkable thing about that onesie, no fine details or special significance that might inspire me to save it. Normally, I would be too superstitious to have ever consciously bought something for a baby that didn't yet exist. But my hopeful mind had other plans, transforming that $5 piece of cotton into something more. While a parade of miniature rompers and t-shirts, dresses and sneakers cycled through those shopping bags over the next few years, the stars-and-fish onesie remained, rooted with meaning. I couldn't bear to part with it, to see another baby wear it. Hope told me to hang on.

My behavior was irrational—largely beyond my control. Hope was often like that for me.

No matter how many times I failed, there wasn't a month that went by that Hope didn't convince me I was pregnant. She probed at my heavy breasts, called out my fatigue, noted the metallic taste of pregnancy on my tongue. She counted forward nine months, again and again, tabulating birthdays; would we have a Leo on our hands? A Sagittarius? Hope informed my dentist and dermatologist about a possible upcoming pregnancy, should we need to skip X-rays or switch to gentler medication. Once, when buying a bridesmaid dress, Hope sent an email asking how they accounted for women whose pregnant bodies changed in the months before the wedding. She was unabashed in her optimism.

Hope had a direct line to my subconscious, too. She made me leave the walls in our guest room bare—don't invest, she insisted knowingly, since it will be a nursery soon enough. Browsing through a furniture store near my office I came upon an overstuffed, impractically white couch that we didn't need. When I disappeared into the cushions, Hope conjured an image of me lounging in that same spot, round belly puncturing the air above. *It's the perfect place to rest an achy, pregnant body,* she whispered. We'll take it, I said aloud.

Hope was persistent, indefatigable, resilient beyond reason. Every single month, when experience and pain and frustration and failure would tell me to do otherwise, I believed. Within days or sometimes hours of an IVF cycle failing, Hope was not only reborn but renewed with full conviction; the most deep-rooted of involuntary reactions, trumpeting the possibility of whatever we were about to try next. Change doctors! Transfer multiple embryos!

Get genetic testing! *It will work!* Dutifully, I did whatever she told me. She was the thing giving me life, after all, so I did whatever it took to keep her going, too.

I wasn't blind about it, though. Or at least I tried not to be. False Hope I had no use for.

Throughout the years I spent trying to get pregnant I was told dozens of stories about infertility that ended happily. So-and-so's boss had gotten pregnant at 44. A friend's co-worker had finally been successful after temporarily relocating for access to better treatment. The reassurances kneaded at my lumpy shoulders, smoothing out the knots. But I also took an odd interest in stories with a different outcome. I started reading a blog written by a woman who was giving up after a 10-years-long struggle with infertility, obsessively scrolling back through her old posts. What was her diagnosis? How did she get here? It felt important to face the grim truth that you could do all of this, want it more than anything, and still walk away without a baby.

When I started seeing a therapist after our third failed IVF, I asked her if she had ever worked with patients dealing with infertility. She said she had. I asked what kinds of outcomes she had seen. She said, plainly, that she had seen it work for some and not for others. It seems obvious now, but I was taken aback. Hearing the unadorned truth, when so many voices were insistent that we would be successful, was a shock. Still, I was grateful. I wanted to acknowledge the raw, painful reality of our situation. I didn't want to delude myself.

Somehow, though, I managed to do exactly that, subverting those same stark truths to underscore the validity of my own Hope. This Hope you see here, I seemed to be trying to prove to myself, this isn't Pollyanna Hope. My Hope is clearer. Different.

I took a strange pride in being realistic about our chances for a baby, so when we had failed enough times that friends and family started giving up on us, I was outraged.

"Have you thought about other options?" they asked (pleaded, really). "Has your doctor recommended you get on adoption lists," they'd ask, pausing before adding, "just in case?"

I recoiled with fury and hurt, defensive of our Hope. In the early days, I resented people's undying conviction that IVF would work for us, a sentiment that to me seemed rosy to the point of being dismissive—proof they didn't get it. And now, at the end, it had come full circle. Now I resented that they had decided it wasn't going to happen.

"Nope," I snapped, "he hasn't said anything about adoption. He still thinks I'll get pregnant."

But then my Hope ran out too.

Our fifth IVF embryo transfer was, in the opinion of all involved, The One. For the first time, we were using genetically-tested embryos—two of them—which both our current and previous doctors believed would be the thing to ultimately work for us. These hearty embryonic stars had every last chromosome intact and would step in to get the job done. They were our Sure Things. Due to various delays—switching clinics, sending the embryos to the lab for testing, recovering from my two surgeries—we transferred them roughly six months after the idea was first proposed.

Which meant that for 180 days, give or take, with the urgency and desperation of IVF at a fever pitch, I waited. Waited as the holidays came and went, while the seasons changed, as we marked birthdays, attended funerals, resolved to get a dog. And in that eternity, in the pauses between each ticking second, Hope stood at her pulpit and delivered her most masterful sermon yet, spreading her gospel, her light, so that she overtook me, soaring out from my heart to the tips of my fingernails, swirling through the curvature of my brain, cascading down through each leg until pooling at my toes. Every inch of me was illuminated with the static electricity of possibility. *I believed!* By the time we transferred those two embryos, Hope had become unrecognizable—she was masquerading as Truth.

This could work.

This should work.

This will work.

And then—it didn't.

Those powerhouse embryos sputtered and flailed and disappeared, absorbed back into the galaxy of my body. Hope, the tenacious force that had encouraged me through every procedure, picked me up after every negative pregnancy test, comforted me as so many friends announced pregnancies of their own—she was gone. Her twinkly vapor was suctioned out of me in a single, shocking gasp. She could not endure that final blow.

Without her, I was lost. She had been the engine behind everything. The belief that the process would eventually work, that I would one day hold our baby in my arms. She had kept me going. If we didn't have Hope, we had nothing. We were done.

After we got the news, Tim and I sat down across from our doctor, our eyes dulled, our nerves sharp. We still didn't have a diagnosis, no explanation for why IVF wasn't working. Fighting what had turned out to be an unknown enemy was destroying us. What a waste this had all been.

Our doctor expressed genuine surprise and disappointment that this last cycle hadn't worked. But, he said, he still believed we would get there. He told us he would be devastated if we gave up. That if we were his family members he would encourage us to keep going. He had a plan, he said. He wanted to biopsy my uterus and present our case to the other doctors in the practice; maybe one of them would think of something he hadn't. He was still optimistic, but he no longer seemed sure that success was imminent. He didn't know how long it would take, so we should settle in for the long haul. Don't give up, he pleaded. What else is there?

His passion was evident. *His* hope meant something, even if I had no more of my own. It seemed unthinkable to continue like this—to choose pain again and again—but the alternative sounded worse.

So, a few weeks after that conversation I walked back into the clinic to begin another IVF cycle—our sixth. Without the effervescence of Hope fizzing inside, I was weighed down. It was a sunny Saturday in the middle of May, but I wore a turtleneck, pulling the neck up over my chin and the sleeves down over my knuckles as I slouched in the chair waiting for my blood work and ultrasound. It was a scene I knew well: This roomful of women, all of us sitting in silence, mindlessly paging through magazines or conversing in low tones with a partner until a name was called and one of us sprang out of our seat.

To be starting again, to be waiting again, it was all so familiar, the only thing changed being me. Still—I was there. I was doing it. Breathing, surviving, trying. I was continuing on in spite of the losses. In the midst of my hopelessness, the realization felt not hope*ful*, exactly, but rooted in something like it.

Plus, there was this: Hope was gone, yes, but she left something behind. There was still a onesie in the back of my closet. I never did let it go.

# Dread

That fifth IVF cycle, those genetically-tested embryos, fertility-wise, felt like the equivalent of playing with a stacked deck. Our doctor was so convinced we would be successful that he initiated near-daily conversations about how many embryos we should transfer. We discussed over email, we had calls, he'd poke his head in when I was having blood drawn in the morning to say, *So what are we doing? What's the plan?* Given that I was only 33, and these were genetically-tested (in my mind, approved, confirmed, nearly certain potential children), his strong recommendation was that we put only one embryo inside me. He told us this again and again, as though his conscience was burdened by some sort of medical prescience. If we transferred two, he said, our odds of conceiving twins were extremely high. For good measure, he often reminded us of the low (but real) odds that one embryo could split in two on its own, in which case we'd have triplets.

Tim and I wanted to be sensible, so we hemmed and hawed, circling the topic over email during the day, and while eating dinner at our kitchen counter at night. We approached it mathematically—weighing the odds of this scenario or that. We also approached it emotionally. We would be transferring the embryos in early April, not having done so since the previous December. There was no pretending that the gap had been anything other than agonizing, not to mention all the months and cycles that had come before. Other than the odd writing project, I still wasn't working, our lives on hold as we pursued this baby with everything we had. We considered the emotional repercussions of another failure—it was our *fifth* transfer, after all—compared with the risks and responsibility and stress of having twins. In the end, at dinner one night, Tim, Mr. Rational of all people, aptly put it like this: "I think if we're honest with ourselves, logic says one but our hearts say two." Yes, I agreed. That was exactly right.

I saw our doctor nearly every morning for monitoring, but he and Tim rarely had a chance to talk. So they arranged a call one night—Tim from our kitchen, our doctor from his car driving home—and the two of them devised a plan. We would use the strongest and the weakest of the four embryos we had remaining. It gave us the security of transferring two, knowing the weaker one had a lesser chance of making it, which undercut the risk for twins. In the end, we hedged.

So that was where our minds were in the weeks leading up to the transfer—one embryo or two, a single baby or twins. Failure was not an option. We were to test on a Saturday, which meant that Tim and I would be together when the results came in. First thing that morning we drove into Manhattan for the blood draw, then turned around and drove back to Brooklyn, to a cozy breakfast spot we'd been wanting to try. I remember the pancakes being good, the sausage too, but I wound up taking half of my meal to-go because I was too restless to know what to do with it.

Back at home we sat beside each other on the couch, my fingers strangling my phone, and waited. When the screen lit up, I launched off the couch and stalked across the apartment. *Would it be one baby or two?* "Hello? This is Amy."

A voice came through on the other end. The nurse was sorry to tell me that my hCG count was only 27; it was a chemical pregnancy. It was over.

Tim had leapt off the couch after me, and stood, watching and listening expectantly. He quickly realized what had happened through the crumpling of my face, the catch in my throat. I was grateful, in the end, that he was there. I didn't have to say the words.

We hugged. I sobbed. We lay back down on the couch, closed our eyes, and fell asleep in a hot tangle. I was certain my doctor would call later; I think he did. It's hard to remember. I ate cold pancakes with my fingers, standing up at the counter. I couldn't process what was happening.

For the first time, I could feel in a deep, guttural way that getting pregnant might not happen for us, that I was not capable of doing this indefinitely. There was only so much we could take.

With the beginning of the end upon us, we attempted to make sense of our lives. A week after receiving those results we got a puppy, Maple, to bring life and love into our home. In therapy, my counselor mentioned we might want to start seriously thinking about surrogacy or adoption. I heard her, but we weren't ready for that, not yet. All along, I had resisted the notion of adoption, because I did not know how to move on from this phase without a *reason*. My brain was grappling with how senseless it all felt, that the inordinate amount of time and effort we were investing was not getting us anywhere, and not one person could offer a single explanation as to why. It was a mystery that defied logic, and I was hell-bent on solving it. If I could somehow make the dots connect, if I could finally *understand*, then I would be able to make peace with it, and, eventually, let go. Only then would I have the capacity to truly consider our other options—adoption, surrogacy, all of it.

Within weeks, the outlines of a plan took shape: We would do a sixth IVF transfer with our two remaining genetically-tested embryos. If that failed, we would do a fresh stimulation and a seventh transfer at the end of the summer. After that, we would be done. There, in the not-too-near, yet not-too-distant future, I could see it: a fixed endpoint.

Meanwhile, I was caught in a swirl of despair. We were not going to have our own biological children; I would never be a mom, at least not in the way I had imagined. Worse, I could now see that all of it was my fault. Those genetically-tested embryos had provided a new clarity: it wasn't a glitch in either of our genes that was responsible for all our failed cycles. Those embryos were fully capable of becoming babies. The onus lay squarely on my body. Whatever happened between the transfer and the pregnancy test, whatever caused those embryos to dissolve into nothingness, that was on me.

In the aftermath of that last round, Tim had written something to me in an email—something I couldn't shake:

*As I was lying in bed throwing a ball up on Saturday night ... my mind started to wander... I have had this image of throwing a ball with my son in our backyard ... we would play catch and we would talk about life, and it just hit me I may never get to do that.*

It was one thing to be the breaker of my own heart. That I could find a way to live with. What was unbearable—unsurvivable—was bringing this upon Tim. The bonehead with the plot to kill me with a frozen turkey; the love of my life. I knew how badly he wanted to have kids, just as I knew how his love—patient, golden, constant—would make their childhoods magical. I could see him on the sidelines at soccer practice, helping our kids learn the game, underscoring the importance of trying hard, of being a good sport. This man who was a finance whiz yet had earnestly once described himself to me as a "triple threat," then looked confused when I asked for clarification on which of his gifts comprised that trio ("is that a real question?" he was incredulous. "Singing, dancing, and acting.") I was wistful imagining him serenading our children with made-up songs in silly voices, the funny dance moves he would perform for them. I could see our kids admiring him, and him teaching them what really mattered. I thought about how he would shine in that role. How he was made for it. And I thought about how I was the reason he wouldn't get to have the life he deserved. It wasn't my choice, but that didn't stop it from being my fault.

Feeling disappointment had brought me to the brink; being a disappointment was pushing me past it. I sat down for my Monday appointment with my therapist and pulled tissue after tissue out of the box as I explained my realization, how those genetically-tested embryos had taught us something new. This—the failure, the pain, the inherent brokenness in our lives, our future—was on me. Kristin listened to my confession, then asked, neutral and measured, "Have you thought about telling Tim all of this?"

I had not. Nor had I imagined she would suggest such a thing. I had hoped my unburdening in the confines of her office would suffice. Maybe she would've even disagreed with me, suggested I not be so hard on myself. But that is not what happened. She did not let me off the hook. She gently encouraged me to tell Tim what I was feeling. "Do you think that is something you would feel comfortable doing?" *No, Kristin, in fact that sounds like the absolute worst thing I can think of.* Out loud I said I guessed so, and walked out of her office with a chunk of dread in the back of my throat.

Could I really acknowledge my greatest shortcoming, my ultimate failure? Because once I called attention to it, then what? Would he still want this life with me? He was certainly painfully aware that we hadn't been able to have a baby. But for me to own it in this way, to accept accountability, to put words to the disappointment he must feel while acknowledging that I was the source of it—that would be downright world-shattering.

Still, once Kristin suggested it, I knew I didn't have a choice: I had to tell him.

The moment came over Memorial Day weekend. Our sixth round of IVF was underway, but we had another week or so until the transfer. With permission to free ourselves from the tether of morning monitoring, we escaped to a tiny ramshackle cottage in the woods a few hours from New York City. We did very little over those few days—cooked dinner on the grill, sat by the glowing gas fireplace in the evenings as Maple rolled around the floor. I remember standing in the rusty, crumbling bathroom, pressing slime-filled whitening trays against my teeth. I had put off the chore month after month, for years now, not wanting to slather my mouth in chemicals when I was trying to grow a healthy baby. But now? Why the fuck not. I was only doing shots to prepare my body for the transfer—there was no embryo inside me yet—and realistically, it looked extremely unlikely that I would ever be pregnant anyway. May as well chug some bleach.

Later that afternoon, Tim and I were having a beer on the back deck watching Maple run around the yard, nibbling grass, chasing bugs. We could hear the trickle of water easing over rocks and sticks from the creek down below, but beyond that the air was empty, daring me to speak. Flies were swirling through slanted sunlight, and with my stomach twisted, my gums on fire, I inhaled deeply and started talking.

I told Tim I was sorry that I wasn't able to make him a father; that I was sorry for letting him down. I told him how deeply it weighed on me, how gravely I felt it, to be disappointing him like this. I told him he *should* be a father, he had every right to be, and how exceptionally well it would suit him. We married knowing we both wanted a family together; I knew this was not the life he signed up for. There was also something I didn't say, my voice couldn't quite get there: That if he wanted to try to pursue that life with someone else, he should do it. Being a father was what he wanted, what he deserved. He should have it. I was too scared to say that part out loud, but I tried to say all the words around it, to hint that I would give him an out in case he needed one.

When I was finished, the sound of the creek returned. It was still there. I was still there. I felt myself in a kind of kinetic mid-air suspension, like a car that has rocketed off a cliff. After a pause, Tim, who had been staring at me, started talking. He had no idea I felt such a burden of responsibility, he said. But it was not my fault, not at all. He did not feel let down by me; this was our problem, we were in it together.

His words were everything I could have hoped to hear. Reassuring, supportive, loving. I was grateful; I felt relief. As I came down from the heart-pounding sensation of heavy words released, we sat there in shaded silence on the porch, afternoon sun drenching the yard. I don't think we ever hugged; it wasn't like that. He might have grabbed my hand, we might have locked eyes, soundlessly acknowledging my exposed vulnerability, our shared sorrow. I might have tried to pull my face into the approximation of a smile, but the closed-mouth kind, lips stitched together, as I did in most pictures from around this time. Burning white teeth inside that no one ever got to see.

# *Acceptance*

As a kid, I fantasized about running away to the woods along the highway that took us out of town, gazing longingly from the car at what lay just beyond the pavement as we drove along the Saw Mill River Parkway south to the Jersey Shore, or north to Upstate New York, our two summer vacation spots. The land stretched up a hill and then disappeared, my sense was that just out of sight it was all thicket and seclusion, like the setting for *The Boxcar Children* books I had stacked up in my bedroom. Visible from the road were intermittent stretches of crumbling stone wall, and endless rows of trees, knit together by a dense canopy of leaves. I envisioned myself tucked beneath the green, where I'd be cool and dry and safe, hidden from the passing cars. There, I imagined, I'd feel comfort and peace, and no one would find me, though I wasn't sure what, exactly, I was looking to escape from.

The thing is, though, when what you want to run from is your body, bolting is not an option. And when infertility got hard, then harder, where was I to go? So I stayed put, dug in. It wasn't until we neared the end that I started planning my escape.

\*\*\*

It doesn't feel true to say that Tim and I made a *decision* to stop trying; the end was born from recognition. A willingness to see what was. After that fifth failed IVF, the thundering, seismic crash of those, I believed, fool-proof, genetically-tested embryos, I found myself at the dining table one morning clicking on an essay about adoption. I'd read and re-read all the other personal stories about infertility on the Resolve website, my eyes refusing to acknowledge this one. Now, for the first time, I noticed. I opened. I read; not exactly with an open heart so much as one that was full of holes.

It was at that same table, possibly even that same day, that the refrain in my head formed, then became a recurring, resounding echo: *My soul is ready to be done.* It emerged from someplace inaccessible, a place that inhabited every cell in my body, that could speak to me even if I could not speak back. A place of deep, personal truth. *My soul is ready to be done.* Sitting there, the stripped-down power of those words resonated, obliterating all the maybes, the what ifs, the voices insisting that I wasn't even 35 and had insurance that would cover IVF for a lifetime, an unlimited amount of tries. My lips traced the words, understanding. I did not have unlimited tries left in me. It was almost over.

\*\*\*

The therapy of acupuncture was as much about being in Deborah's presence as it was the magic of her needles. I found healing in her smiling eyes, her knowing, *hi there* when she greeted me, her effortless connection to all that was fraught about my struggles. She exuded a profound humanness that took the chill out of my otherwise clinical daily life.

"I can't keep doing this." My words were devoid of emotion, simply a thudding expression of truth. Deborah stood, leaning against a table, nodding solemnly in agreement. "None of it is working. I mean, obviously, but—all of a sudden, I am finally seeing clearly that this is not going to happen." I hated every word I was saying, and I hated how much I meant it. "It is unbearable to think that after all of this we're going to walk away with nothing, but I can't shake this feeling that my soul is just ready to be done."

Besides Tim, Deborah had been my closest ally in this process. She had seen and heard it all, every last torturous detail. In her, I found the rare sort of intimacy that can only exist between patient and practitioner; she was a kindred spirit, as well as someone uniquely without context. She'd never met Tim, hadn't known me before all of this, had no expectations informed by who I used to be, as to who I should be now, or whether the me who was so single-minded about getting pregnant made sense. This me was all she knew, and I found an unencumbered sense of freedom in that.

"I understand," she said, looking pained. "So, what are you two thinking?" I looked down into my hands. "Well, the good news—I mean, there's no good news, but you know what I mean—is that Tim and I are aligned on what we want to do. We're planning to do a round with our last two genetically-tested embryos, and then we'll do one last stimulation and transfer after that." My voice hesitated. "I want to be able to walk away knowing I left it all on the field, so I'm going to try every last thing I can think of. But then," I paused, still struggling to give the words air, "we're planning to be done."

We were still for a moment, the air settling in the room, ambient noise from the street below floating through the window. "Ok," Deborah said, before adding, with all the quiet conviction I was lacking, "I like that plan. I want to hear more and we can keep talking once you're on the table, but why don't we get to it? Shall I work on your back today? Let out your shoulders and really try to release some tension?" I nodded. Soon I was face down, my bare shoulders peeking out from beneath a white sheet. "Do you mind if I remove your necklace?" Deborah asked, once she returned; had I not been so out of sorts I would have remembered to take it off myself. "It's beautiful," her voice was disembodied, but we'd spent enough time together in this room that I could place her in it, picture her admiring the necklace before letting it dangle into a little dish. "Is there any special meaning behind it?" The gold chain was impossibly delicate, like grains of salt on a string, with an arrow, slim and crisp, set in the middle. There was no significance to it, I explained, my words muffled by the face rest. Just something pretty that I liked. Deborah paused for a moment, not entirely willing to accept that answer. "Well," she said, "maybe it's pointing you in the right direction."

***

"Hey," Tim said, dropping his keys on the counter and crouching down to Maple's level. "How was she today?" He rubbed behind her ears and smiled as her eager pink tongue slipped up his cheek. "She was fine. I mean, she's exhausting, I'm walking her like seven times a day and still cleaning her shit off the floor." I paused, pierced by the sharpness of my own words. "But she was good, I guess." I tried to walk it back. "I'm just exhausted."

This had become the tenor of so many conversations between Tim and me. Moody and tense, one if not both of us snapping. Occasionally, we escalated into full-out hostility. One recent Saturday morning the wait for monitoring at the clinic was especially long: one hour, then two, then three. As the rage bubbled, my nerves scratched raw, I turned to Tim beside me, ignoring the fact that the place was packed with patients, and for what reason I can't even recall I screamed at him with unexpected fury: *Just leave!*

We were two people with an abundant supply of sadness and anger and no outlet, and so it all pooled into standing water between us, its surface toxic, muddied, so much obscured beneath the surface. "Well, I'll obviously walk her twice tonight and again in the morning," Tim offered. I nodded distractedly.

"I was thinking more about Northern California," I said, changing the subject, "and honestly, I think it could be really good. If you got transferred to the San Francisco office, and we lived outside the city, maybe Davis, I was thinking?" The extent of my knowledge of Davis, California came from a blogger I'd been following for the past year or two. She was raising her two young kids there and documented her family's very photogenic life on her site: their dreamy house renovation, homemade cakes for the kids' birthdays, intimate dinner parties with friends, outdoorsy travels to Big Sur and Lake Tahoe.

In tandem with our marathon binges of the show, *Parenthood*, which sold us on the allure of nearby Berkeley, it wasn't a stretch for either Tim or me to picture this next iteration of our life. Treatment would be ending soon, and with the fight phase nearly behind us, taking flight seemed the only way forward. We'd live in a quaint California bungalow, I imagined, or maybe a ranch. I could see the drought-tolerant plants in the yard, sun-drenched rooms filled with mid-century décor, all of it a comfortable 3,000 miles from our heartache and failure and trauma. We'd breathe fresh air and spend time outdoors, walk on wide, anonymous streets and take off on road trips with our super-chill new West Coast friends. Maybe I'd even start wearing hats; people in California always seemed to have very cool and extensive collections of hats. The other side of the country seemed a convenient place to settle for a couple who'd be content to visit their East Coast families maybe once a year but sit out the rest of the roster of holidays to avoid being surrounded by other people's children.

"I agree," Tim said, giving oxygen to my hope for our future. "I don't know much about Davis, but you don't have to convince me about Northern California, I've always wanted to live there."

"The only other possibility I thought could be interesting," I continued, "and I don't know if this is even possible, but if you could take a leave of absence from work, we could travel for a while, like, six months or something, and then come back to New York and kind of re-group from there. I just feel like I need a break from all of this. I can't just give up on the possibility of having children on, like, a Tuesday, and then go back to what life used to look like on a Wednesday."

That was the thing: if there was to be a future when we could maybe, possibly, be ok, it would have to be separated from our present moment by time and space, the more the better. It was only by thinking about that space, that emptiness, that I could envision anything beyond it. In our current existence, the ghosts of infertility were everywhere, hidden in the rumpled sheets of our bed, tucked in the shopping bag in the back of my closet, embedded into my actual skin. I couldn't wipe it all clean, but I could do my best to run, to outpace the pain.

And then, I was sure, with physical and temporal distance to make us whole, we would approach our next decision with clear eyes. We might pursue adoption, or consider surrogacy, or feel peace with not having children at all. I genuinely couldn't guess where our path would lead us from here, but I didn't intend to carry the baggage of my pain and disappointment and stress if I could help it. If we decided to adopt, then I wanted that choice to be distinct from this phase; something I arrived at, not settled on. A decision made from joy and hope, not despair. I needed to grieve this fully before genuinely wanting that.

"I don't think I can just take a leave of absence from work, I mean I'm pretty sure that's not an option," Tim seemed stressed by the idea. "But I like the sound of traveling and I agree that we need some sort of break from all this. I don't know, I'm open to it but let's just keep talking."

Tim's relative, if not overwhelming, receptiveness, the feeling that we were coming up with the vague outline of a plan, felt like soothing milk on a burn. I'd been set ablaze by something my therapist had put out there in our last session— a kind of warning. In light of this last failed cycle, she thought it would be a good idea to start considering some different possibilities. What else might we try? What alternatives to IVF might we consider? "I just want you to start thinking about how else this might look for you. Because the longer you continue on your present path, the greater the possibility that you do irreparable damage to your relationship."

Those words—*irreparable damage*—had been raging inside of me. I wanted this child, this family, beyond reason. But not at the expense of Tim and me. Three out of the four years of our marriage had been spent trying and failing to have a baby. If we kept at it, we were on track to burn the whole damn thing to the ground.

***

My sister and I stood in the side yard of our childhood home, the brink-of-summer sun warming our faces. "So, that's what we're thinking," I concluded. "Moving to California, or else setting off on some sort of long-term travel." I could usually anticipate Stephanie's reactions, but today, it was anyone's guess what I would hear in response. Would she be devastated that I was planning to disappear? Say that these options seemed a little extreme? "Veed, I love it," she was smiling, an exhale easing across her face. "I think that sounds so, so good. I'm so happy to hear it. Seeing you accept it really brings me peace."

The thread of acceptance had been woven through so many conversations with both my sister and Deborah, who for so long had been encouraging me toward letting go. It wasn't the unhelpful sort of letting go they were proposing, the eye-rolling kind that instructs you to "just relax," or to "have fun with it, it'll happen when you're not even trying!" (Can we all please agree to stop saying that?) Or worse, advising we quit the whole thing. This was a different suggestion altogether: to find a way to continue on, to keep trying, but to surrender the fight. Women struggling to get pregnant often refer to themselves as "infertility warriors," but what if I stopped battling my body, ceased my efforts to force it into submission?

That prospect seemed a riddle I could never quite solve: How could I exert effort, give everything that infertility treatment required, sacrifice, suffer, and *care* so very deeply, while simultaneously allowing things to be what they were? It felt paradoxical: Give all you've got to change things but accept what it is.

Now, though, in this moment of all-out exhaustion, as we set off on our sixth cycle of IVF, I had finally released my grip. I was showing up to appointments, yet I was done fighting. I had allowed other ideas—adoption, moving, surrogacy, traveling, life without children—to seep into my mind. I hadn't achieved acceptance by any means, but I was willing to consider other outcomes. After so many years of clawing my way through this thing, my balled-up fists were beginning to unclench. In finally acknowledging that I would never have any real, meaningful control over my body, I would at last regain control over my life.

"I mean, I have no idea what I'll do if this really doesn't work," I said quickly back to my sister, lest she think I was somehow ok with all of this. "I haven't accepted it. But—I'm getting closer."

***

It was both depressing and liberating to be undergoing IVF with resignation, or, more truthfully, not giving a fuck, all but sure that once again, it wouldn't work. Perhaps in rebellion, I decided I wanted to have a lone drink to mark my 34th birthday, which fell just a couple of days after our final two embryos were deposited into my uterus. I emailed the nurse for clearance:

*I never drink alcohol after a transfer, but my birthday is on Friday and I kind of want to have a beer/wine. Just one! But I don't want to do anything dumb or irresponsible. Anyway, just wanted to see how you felt about that :)*

It was one measly drink, I figured. And, honestly, we both knew how this would be playing out. To my surprise, though, she wasn't having it:

*Happy birthday!! I would really not recommend having anything to drink because you are considered pregnant. Sparkling grape juice ha.*

I responded with joking nonchalance, letting her know it was no big deal:

*Haha ok got it! I will get wild with my sparkling grape juice :)*

My lighthearted reply, however, was bullshit. I cried, shed actual tears over being denied one stupid drink. Anticipating this second IVF birthday, a full year since our first round, reflecting on the shock and loss and loneliness of these last 365 days, not to mention the two agonizing years before that, I was outraged and overcome by the injustice of being denied a sip of alcohol. The loss of one fucking beer on my birthday turned out to be one loss too many.

Still, I would do what she said. I would see this through to the bitter end. We were almost there.

\*\*\*

My birthday fell on a Friday, landing with a thud. Tim was working that day, but in the evening we drove down to the Jersey Shore, the woods along the highway flush with spring, beckoning to me through the open window. Our night was quiet; we must have eaten dinner, watched TV. There was a single picture of me taken that day, lying beside Maple on the couch, the hood of my grey sweatshirt pulled over my head, my eyes closed. It is not an image of a woman at ease, a woman who has found peace. Rather, one who has attained stillness. A woman in submission.

The next morning, I awoke feeling a little lighter, with the weight and expectations of my actual birthday behind me. When Tara, Desi, and his boyfriend arrived with their smiles and spirit, I felt lighter still. They brought distraction and laughter, and I took solace in their presence, their conversation, at breathing the briny air, staring at the water and beyond it to the horizon. There was some kind of future out there, even if we didn't know what it was.

They also brought cake, a homemade masterpiece of layers and frosting and symmetry, and once night fell, we prepared to dig in. Four voices joined to sing to me, the song just the same as it had been since the day I was born, and I hovered over my beautiful cake, round like cycles and seasons and beginnings and endings, the candles flickering against my face like a sky full of stars. The group looked at me expectantly as I turned inward, chanting a well-worn refrain in my head. My one and only wish. I pursed my lips, pushed out air, and silenced the flames into oblivion.

## Interlude: A note to the reader

I felt compelled to write an infertility story that was not defined by outcome—"a conception story" or "an adoption story"—but by the raw emotion and hardship and absurdity of the plight itself. A book about the *experience*, The difficult truth is that as we make our way through, none of us knows how our infertility story will end; in reflection of that, the core of the story concludes here, suspended in the unknown.

Except, of course, there *is* an outcome to my story. The way it all played out for Tim and me is detailed on the ensuing pages. But infertility is a profoundly delicate business, and my aim is not to thrust that upon anybody. To learn of another woman's outcome is something we all deserve to feel a degree of control over, or at the very least not be blindsided by. So please, take care, and read on only when and if you are moved to do so.

# *Afterward*

It's hard to know why I tested at home despite having long ago stopped testing at home. Maybe I was bored, or maybe I was emboldened, someone who so wholly did not give a fuck, having gotten five consecutive IVF nos on the heels of three IUI nos, which came after the Clomid nos and all the unmedicated nos before that. Maybe I just wanted to get this no out of the way already. Or maybe something in me felt that on this day, for whatever reason, it might finally be a yes. All I know is that within minutes of when I dug up an old plastic stick in the linen closet and brought it into the bathroom, I found myself staring at two parallel pink lines: the first positive home pregnancy test of my life.

I placed it on the counter, then picked it up again a second later. I looked at it, looked away, then looked back. I smiled. Big and full and mystified and uncertain. I turned on the water to take a shower and began to undress, though my instinct was to stay exactly where I was, as if moving the wrong way or stepping beyond the space I was in might somehow break the spell. Under the spray I closed my eyes, droplets running down my face, then pulled back the curtain to peek at the lines again. When I wrapped myself in a towel, they were still there.

After so many years of struggle there was no way to simply accept a positive home pregnancy test at face value. I knew better than to weep or dance or shout or celebrate. Still, something in me had expanded. I had been so sure that sheer will was the one way I could ever force this moment into being. But what if, all along, the opposite had been true? What if in strangling my way through this process, holding on with every ounce of my strength, I hadn't allowed space for the alchemy of existence to break through? As I sat waiting for Tim to come home, it was as if I'd been cracked open by possibility, air rushing through me at the speed of light.

We chatted for a few minutes before I knew what to say. "So," I dragged out the word. "I tested today." We stared at each other for a moment before irrepressible grins spread across both of our faces. "Wow. Ok. And?" Tim asked. "I mean it says it's positive. It's on the bathroom counter, go look." Tim jumped off the couch, incredulous, then returned within seconds, smiling even bigger than before. "So, like, is that accurate?" He, too, was guarding against the joy. "I think so. It should be." I paused. "I've literally never seen a positive test before." We stood face to face, then encircled each other with our arms. "Well, no matter what, it's a great sign." He thought a little more. "Should you take another one?" I pulled back. "That was the only test I have left. But I'm going to walk to CVS in the morning and get more."

I was the first person in the store, striding down the aisle. Back at home, several different types of tests all returned the same result.

When I walked into the clinic on Thursday morning, I ran into my doctor in the hallway. "Hey," he said. "Did you test?" It was a funny thing to ask; why would I have tested when in theory today was the earliest a pregnancy could be detected? "I actually did, I never test but for some reason I did." I was reluctant to even say it out loud. "And?" He was expectant. "It said it was positive," I replied, with obvious hesitation. My doctor looked skeptical. "Was the line faint or dark?" I shrugged my shoulders. "It was pretty dark. And I took a bunch, they were all positive." He smiled back for the first time. "All right. Well, let's see what the blood says."

The call from the nurse came later that day and everything I needed to hear was there in the lilt in her voice, the bursting emotion with which she said my name. "Amy? I have your results here, and I am so happy to tell you that you are pregnant." I gasp-choked. "No," I said, with a feeble tremble, the whole world rearranging itself around me. "I am?"

I hung up the phone and hugged Tim, my shoulders heaving.

\*\*\*

I remained somewhat cautious, especially early on, but for the most part, I didn't feel the need to hold my breath throughout the pregnancy. All of my trauma existed on the other side, the before of the stubbornness of my body, its rejection of sperm and embryos, its absolute refusal to allow anything in. Once I crossed over into pregnancy, my instinct was to trust—not merely my body, but this baby. If this person was somehow strong enough to break through, then I felt sure that he or she would make it all the way. It was my belief in this person, this tiny dynamo, that brought me peace.

When our baby arrived, thirteen days and a few years late, it was Tim who was the one to tell me, soft and misty-eyed: *you have a daughter.* This person, the one—the *only* one—who was able to dig in and hold on, she was a girl. *Hazel.*

In those early days together, this beautiful, perfect human sprawled across my chest, one cheek pressed against my skin, my own eyes closed in blissful depletion, I thought about something I had read in one of my pregnancy books, one of those marvels of biology that nearly defies belief, that female babies are born with all of their eggs already inside of them. I looked at Hazel, alert, tenacious, so very determined to have gotten here. Someday, should she choose to pursue the path to motherhood and have the good fortune of it working out, the eggs that would one day become her children would have already been there inside of her, when she was still inside of me, as though we were a series of miniature Russian dolls, each colorful wooden orb encapsulating the next, connected by cells and spirit long before we would ever meet.

When Tim and I first started trying, getting pregnant was an expectation. I took it for granted: my right as a woman. Yet when I really think about it, the way a million tiny parts must align, the innumerable complex, interconnected systems that have to work in tandem to make such a thing possible, I am left speechless by the implausibility of it all.

Setting out to create a life, attempting to unleash the sort of infinitesimal spark capable of crackling and blazing into a human being, is perhaps the purest thing any of us can do. But pure is not the same as easy: the endeavor arduous, or effortless, we don't get to choose. In the end, I experienced both. When Hazel was a toddler, we went back to our doctor for a seventh go at IVF. The result of that round—improbably, *unimaginably*—was twins. From two untested, minimally developed embryos came a full-fledged boy and girl. Asa and Georgia. My unlikely, impossible family, formed, as that beautiful line goes; *slowly first, and then all at once.*

\*\*\*

There is no forgetting infertility, but twins make it visible to the world in a way that endures. *Do they run in your family?* strangers like to ask. *They don't,* I say, neglecting to elaborate, not quite sure how to explain them, remnants of the shame I used to feel resurfacing from down deep. People will surely ask that question for the rest of my life; I wonder if the shame will stick around just as long.

There is guilt too, to be sure. I am one of the lucky ones, emerging from the depths of this mess with three children, human beings who exist solely because we had the financial means to try again and again and again. I'm not quite sure what any of us is supposed to do with that.

I've long struggled to make sense of the whole story, the enraging extent to which it didn't work, coupled with the improbable extent to which it eventually did. The unfathomable mystery of it all. To reconcile the me I was before all of this, with the me who turned her world upside down and herself inside out to try to get pregnant, with the me who exists today, the one who is three peoples' mom.

It's been years since yellow bikini me, under the spell of sunlight shimmering off the Aegean, sat conjuring a million possibilities for how things would turn out for Tim and me, all the great mysteries of my life. Looking back, I see that I pictured those unknowns less as anything genuinely mystifying and more as a series of inevitabilities, a bunch of uninspired either/ors. City or suburbs. Boys or girls.

It is only now that I grasp a distinction, that if I was to re-order the words, juxtapose *life* with *mystery* ever so differently, it would allow for a shift in meaning, one that would bring me closer to the truth of how things wound up actually playing out. The *great mysteries of my life*, as I contemplated them, could be guessed at, chased down with breathless anticipation. They were questions I could dream up and answers I could easily imagine. *Life's great mysteries*, on the other hand, are something different. It's a category reserved for all that can never be explained.

Back then I couldn't have comprehended the difference, because as far as I'd ever known, the one and only thing to do with a mystery was to solve it. Episodes of *Dateline*, my endless stacks of Nancy Drew, the copy of *Gone Girl* I held in my hands there on that dock in Turkey. Every one of those mysteries, whether plucked from reality or pure fiction, provided the satisfaction of tracing details, from clue to clue, until a conclusion where, at last, everything added up.

It took the most profound and personal mystery of my life— one involving my body, my fertility, my family, my identity—to shatter that belief. The truth is that I don't get to understand what went so wrong inside of me. I'll never be able to explain how Hazel, after everything, broke through, or why, not long after, Asa and Georgia sprang into being, determined to enter this world together. None of it makes sense. What I know now is this; it doesn't have to.

See, in freeing myself from the satisfaction of an answer, I've finally allowed myself to be dazzled by the question. To consider the possibility that the mystery, in itself, is the thing of wonder. That perhaps the ultimate point is not to investigate or inspect, to uncover all the facts, needle through to get to the heart of what *happened*. Achieve clarity on what it all *means*. Perhaps the pleasure is not in the solving, but in the beholding. Perhaps sometimes, all we're meant to do is leave the thing whole, admire it for what it is.

Because a certain kind of mystery, one that dances beyond the realm of the knowable, that challenges the limits of what can be explained, is something special. It is a marvel.

All the questions that upended my life are still out there, dangling in the vast emptiness of space and time, littered among the stars. But my searching is done. As it turns out, beyond explanation, beyond sense, even beyond dreams, exists something better than an answer. It is worth believing in.

# *Acknowledgments*

To all the women in all the waiting rooms; I see you. I am you. Mine is one infertility story among millions, and it is not lost on me what a privilege it is to get to tell it. My deepest hope is that you recognize yourself somewhere on these pages and feel a little bit less alone.

I am exceptionally grateful to the team at Unsolicited Press for seeing something worthwhile in my manuscript, and for affording me the time and resources and expertise to transform it into the book that it's become.

Thank you to the journal editors who believe that women's stories matter, and who felt compelled to say *yes*. Earlier versions of "Hope" and "Disappointment" appeared in *Motherwell* and *Literary Mama*, respectively, and those opportunities allowed me to begin to share my story.

I am indebted to the professionals-turned-friends who got me through the most painful and lonely moments of infertility. Deborah Stotzky, Kristin Long, my doctor and his entire team of technicians and nurses—you each embodied the distinction between giving care and *caring*. It makes all the difference.

I don't have an MFA, but I received an education in writing and storytelling as a young editor at the women's magazines of the aughts. Among the many exceptional women I was lucky enough to work alongside was Paula Derrow, who years later became my first editor on this project. Her insights and brilliance helped shape my words and I am so grateful for all the ways she made them better.

I am fortunate to have a chorus of friends and early readers who have supported me, believed in me, and never lost faith in the possibility of what this project could become. Every person who read an essay, met me for coffee, celebrated the wins, lamented the losses, and treated this book like it was real long before it actually was—I have so much gratitude for you. Thank you especially to Desi Gallegos, Sheila Monaghan, Tara Nugent, Jessie Blackhall, Cristina Tudino, Alex Bernath, Malinda Goldberger, Jess Sindler, Lee Helland, Anne Pardes, and Sasha Gordon. I am better for your friendship and this book is better for your wisdom.

Thank you to my mom, to whom I attribute my love of reading, and my dad, to whom I attribute my love of writing—I've only ever wanted to make you proud. To my sister, whose depth and goodness have shaped so much of who I am, and whose support sustains me always. And to my grandfather, who inspires me still. We're a long way from "Grandma's Kitchen" but, Gramps—we did it!

To Tim, first reader, true partner, triple threat for the ages; your belief in me, and your understanding of what matters, make all the difference. I'm so grateful for your openness to sharing this part of our life, and for every single thing you've done in support of me and this book.

Finally, to Hazel and Asa and Georgia—the ones we were meant for. The best part of this story—this life—is you.

# An Interview with Amy

Amy Gallo Ryan's debut book cuts deep with honesty and heart, exploring personal and universal themes with clarity and grace. In this interview, Amy shares insight into her writing habits, the challenges of putting deeply personal stories on the page, and what keeps her motivated—offering readers a glimpse into both her creative process and the mind behind the work.

**Do you have a writing routine or ritual? If so, what is it?**

I'm either not writing or obsessively writing. When the latter happens I lose track of hours at my computer, send emails to myself on my phone when I have to step away, and then rush back to my laptop in bed at night. I have a tendency to hyper focus on perfecting one section over just getting words down on the page, so when I was in the thick of trying to complete the book I would set a daily word count goal. It helped me keep moving forward instead of picking apart what was already there. One essential part of my writing routine is that I must also be reading, that balance in my brain between input and output is critical.

This quote from Julie Buntin, who wrote the novel *Marlena*, really sums up how I feel about the process: "Writing, in my experience, is a self-defined category, this deeply personal mental state, more like a place that I'm constantly trying to fight my way to than an activity." Writing feels like a place to me. And when I'm there it's where I live.

**How do you handle writer's block?**

I get up and walk away—take a shower, go outside, and hope that changing my physical location in the world shakes something loose.

**What's the most surprising thing you've learned about yourself through writing?**

So much of what I understand about myself I've learned through writing. Whatever that quote is, I don't write to tell what I know, I write to figure it out.

**What's the best piece of advice you've ever received about writing?**

Just keep going.

**What's your favorite part of the writing process?**

Discovering how I feel or what I think. And the high of stringing together a precise sequence of words that manage to so completely capture the essence of what you're trying to convey. I am forever seeking The Truth, and there is no better feeling than when you find the words for it.

**What's one book you wish you had written and why?**

*The Empathy Exams* by Leslie Jamison. It's a masterpiece full of depth and insight. She articulates something profound about what it means to be human that feels somehow both familiar and revelatory.

**How do you handle criticism and negative reviews?**

This is my first book so I am bracing myself for all of it. Having endured a multi-heartbreak querying and submission process I am well versed in rejection, though I will say that this book is so intensely personal, it never quite got easier. I've asked my therapist to please not go on vacation right around my pub date!

**What do you hope readers take away from your books?**

A sense of connection. A feeling of being seen. That none of us is alone.

**Do you listen to music while you write? If so, what kind?**

I don't, but the bulk of this book was written during the pandemic when my husband and I were both sitting at desks in our bedroom. He was on calls for the entirety of the day talking about global supply chain delays, while I was trying to put words to the depths of our infertility experience. Even as I recall it now, it's hard to believe that moment really happened. Music probably would have been preferable!

**How do you decide on the titles of your books?**

Titles are *so* hard. This book initially had a different title, and then in the winter of 2022 I did a substantial revise, and once the book changed somewhat it felt like the title should too. My friend Sheila and I were brainstorming over text, and she mentioned how she always responded to titles that were phrases: *I Was Told There'd Be*

*Cake, This Will Only Hurt a Little.* She asked me if there was anything along those lines that could work, maybe something that doctors frequently said, and I gasped and typed: *You May Feel a Bit of Pressure,* followed by a lot of exclamation points. It was already a line in the book, but it took my friend asking the right question to recognize that it should also be the title.

# *About the Author*

Amy Gallo Ryan is a Brooklyn-based writer and former magazine editor whose work has appeared in *Elle, Cosmopolitan, Self* and *Real Simple*, among other publications. Her personal essays have been published on *Motherwell, Literary Mama* and *MER Literary. You May Feel a Bit of Pressure*, an infertility memoir-in-essays, is her first book.

*Photo credit: Beowulf Sheehan*

## About the Press

Unsolicited Press is based out of Portland, Oregon and focuses on the works of the unsung and underrepresented. As a womxn–owned, all–volunteer small publisher that doesn't worry about profits as much as championing exceptional literature, we have the privilege of partnering with authors skirting the fringes of the lit world. We've worked with emerging and award–winning authors such as Sommer Schafer, Amy Shimshon–Santo, Brook Bhagat, Mari Matthias, and Amy Baskin.

Learn more at Unsolicitedpress.com. Find us on Twitter and Instagram at @UnsolicitedP.